THE BEST 100 WEB SITES FOR HR PROFESSIONALS

BOOKS BY JOHN McCARTER & RAY SCHREYER

Employer's Guide to Recruiting on the Internet
Recruit and Retain the Best
The Best 100 Web Sites for HR Professionals

Books in the CareerSavvy Series™:

Anger and Conflict in the Workplace
100 Top Internet Job Sites
101 Hiring Mistakes Employers Make
The 100 Best Web Sites for HR Professionals
The Difficult Hire
Recruit and Retain the Best
Savvy Interviewing
The Savvy Resume Writer

The Best 100
Web Sites for
HR Professionals

RAY SCHREYER & JOHN MCCARTER

IMPACT PUBLICATIONS
Manassas Park, Virginia

Library of Congress Cataloging-in-Publication Data

Schreyer, Ray, 1958—
    The best 100 web sites for HR professionals / Ray Schreyer & John McCarter.
      p. cm.—(The career savvy series)
    Includes index.
    ISBN 1-57023-130-3 (alk. paper)
      1. Personnel management—Computer network resources. 2. Internet (Computer network) I. Title: Best one hundred web sites for HR professionals. II. McCarter, John. III. Series.

HF5549.A27 S37 2000
025.06'6583—dc21   99-089508

Publisher: For information on Impact Publications, including current and forthcoming publications, authors, press kits, bookstore, and submission requirements, visit Impact's Web site: *www.impactpublications.com*

Publicity/Rights: For information on publicity, author interviews, and subsidiary rights, contact the Public Relations and Marketing Department: Tel. 703/361-7300 or Fax 703/335-9486.

Sales/Distribution: Bookstore sales are handled through Impact's trade distributor: National Book Network, 15200 NBN Way, Blue Ridge Summit, PA 17214, Tel. 1-800-462-6420. All other sales and distribution inquiries should be directed to the publisher: Sales Department, IMPACT PUBLICATIONS, 9104 Manassas Dr., Suite N, Manassas Park, VA 20111-5211, Tel. 703/361-7300, Fax 703/335-9486, or *careersavvy@impactpublications.com*

Book design by Kristina Ackley
Layout by Stacy Noyes

Contents

Acknowledgements

Ray Schreyer

I would first like to thank my wife Gayle for allowing me to once again go off on the journey of writing a book. Hopefully this time I was able to find a better balance between this project and other pursuits. I will always cherish your constant love and support.

A great thanks to my friends and colleagues at Little & Associates. I am blessed to be working around some of the most fertile minds and creative spirits on this earth. Additionally, I am privileged to be among some of the most talented, dedicated, and fun HR professionals. Thanks Grace, Tanya, Susan, Rebekka, Linda, and Kristen. I will forever cherish our friendships and working relationship.

Once again I wish to thank my partner in crime John McCarter. I can't believe we are doing this again – for the third time! I think we have both learned the lesson: never say never again.

John McCarter

This is a special acknowledgement to the students, team members, and coaches who have worked with me during the past twenty-two years of consulting to improve productivity, to develop training programs, to define work responsibilities, and general to develop a continuing passion for human growth and achievement. I often learned more than I taught and I shared as much as I could with others. Some contributed more than others did, but naming them would short change the energy and imagination of them all. To list only a very few of several thousand would take too much credit away from the earnest efforts of the others.

But a special thanks must go to my wife, Sue, whose challenging work with the autistic in North Carolina is a continuing source of inspiration. She brings her incredible patience home and humors my ongoing efforts to capture my experience in writing. Her insights are always incisive and her perspectives on human accomplishments are more generous than my own.

INTRODUCTION

This book is designed to be a handy tool for human resource professionals, one that will earn a special location for itself beside your computer. It is a road map to the wonders of the Internet for those who are hungry to explore the information buffet but more than a little uncertain about where to start. Too many new users are simply stunned by both the quantity of useful data available and the frequent difficulty in finding the specific knowledge they seek.

To expedite your text searches in this book, we have divided the one hundred best Internet sites for HR professionals into major categories. There is some ambivalence in those definitions because of the habit of web site designers to try to be everything to everyone. The categories are:

- General
- Professional
- HR Tools
- Legal and Regulatory
- Recruiting
- Relocation
- OD/Change Management/Teams
- Salary Administration
- Training/Career Development
- Benefits

For each site, there will be a small screen shot of its home page, a brief description of its scope and character, and a features list. Its title and web site address will be in the heading. This data will often not be a comprehensive summary of web site contents, but should in most cases allow you to make a quick and accurate assessment of its utility for your current needs. We have tried to be both succinct and fair in our descriptions of the sites. Often the sheer size and coverage of the sites have made that a special challenge.

To a certain extent, we exercised some broad discretion on the selection of the one hundred top sites. Those that were otherwise very useful, but were inordinately hard to use or callously rude to the typical user, were summarily discarded from the selection.

Whenever possible, we identify those sites that expect a membership, fee, subscription, or other consideration in exchange for using significant parts of their site. The 100 listed are either completely free or offer significant utility in those portions of their sites that require nothing but your eager interest. Many of the sites either have an obvious commercial interest in impressing you with their data and insights, or have government or university funding. We did not screen sites by their crass self-interest, but by their discretion by making the services offered of sufficient value to attract continued loyalty.

One caution is suggested about the more extensive portals. The selection of linked sites does not always allow consistent monitoring of their content or continued existence. If you reach an awkward dead end, the fault probably lies with site management, not your telephone lines, computer, or software. Too often, a decision is made to discontinue a web site service, and the site managers simply take it down from their computers and neglect to tell any of the sites to which they are linked. The chief consolation of their callous abandonment is that their content was likely to be as defective as their manners.

We recommend that as you survey this book for useful resources, that you add the more promising ones to the "Favorite Places" or other special list on your browser software. You may also choose to identify sites on your personal manager software to be routinely accessed and reviewed daily, weekly, monthly or some other convenient schedule.

We also request your thoughtful contributions to future issues. If some of the sites listed were of marginal value to you, or if you discover others whose excellence recommends them for addition to future editions of this book, we would appreciate hearing from you. As more human resource professionals become excited by the communications possibilities of the Web, we can imagine future editions of this book that either contain more sites or at least a top 100 group with enhanced value to our readers. Your comments and suggestions will receive serious consideration but we cannot promise a personal reply.

Our earnest hope is that in utilizing this book, you will discover some new insight or critically useful data every time you take a plunge in the Internet's sea of information. That has been our experience and our special delight in writing this book. The human resource profession is both cursed and blessed by the changing environments in which the most valuable assets of any organization are expected to perform. We wish you every success in managing the changes that impact them today, and in anticipating and preparing for those that will inevitably come.

THE BEST 100 WEB SITES FOR HR PROFESSIONALS

1

BENEFITS INTERNET SITES

The benefits section has a limited number of sites, but they either encompass directly or provide convenient links to all the concepts, data, and breaking news about the complex and frequently changing world of employment benefits. In these sites you can fathom the details of federal law and regulations, and explore the broad expanse of commercial benefit management resources.

If benefits are a mundane pursuit, it is because those human resource professionals who care have abandoned the field to compassion-challenged accountants and corporate executives who think that the only barrier between themselves and success are greedy employees. The sound technical knowledge one can find in these web sites can no more give one a heart than the Wizard of Oz could, but HR pros with the necessary equipment may discover that employees with a reasonable benefits package spend more of their time focused on the job and have a much stronger motivation to excel.

AMERICAN SOCIETY OF PENSION ACTUARIES

The ASPA site is targeted toward private pension professionals. There is some obvious overlap with the American Compensation Association, but the ASPA has a tighter, actuarial focus on private retirement plans and their administration. The data in this site will probably tell you as much (or more) about pensions as you want to know without getting a professional degree. There is also a strong involvement in lobbying the federal government on related legislation and regulations. The site also outlines the educational opportunities for HR personnel who want to develop skills and insights in this area.

Standard Features:

- Publication lists
- Membership opportunities
- Excellent site design, easy navigation
- Conference listings
- Outstanding links to related sites
- Certification opportunities
- Membership explanations
- Comprehensive tracking of legislation supported

www.aspa.org

BENEFITSLINK

The BenefitsLink site is a comprehensive resource for HR professionals for whom the specialty is a priority. Two characteristics distinguish the site—the abundance of topics covered and the high quality of Web site design. If the professional articles don't cover the issues with which you are concerned, you have the option of either posting a specific question or submitting your authoritative explanation of the subject. In addition to easy to understand menus, the site provides a search engine to assist newcomers in finding the data or insights they need.

Standard Features:

- Targeted professional jobs site for employers and job candidates
- Benefits library, including state and federal publications
- Links to many additional resources
- An email directory of benefits professionals
- Q & A columns on relevant topics
- Invitations to publish on their site
- Software listing
- Professional resource listing, consultants, etc.
- Employee benefits bookstore
- Listing of free publications
- Conferences and other professional events listed

www.benefitslink.com

EMPLOYEE BENEFIT NEWS

The online edition of *Employee Benefit News* provides all the information contained in the tabloid plus several additional features such as discussion lists, conference schedules, and document bank containing the text of speeches and laws regarding benefits and HR management. The Web site is well designed and easy to read. The homepage is packed with useful information and this site should be a weekly if not daily read for HR professionals involved in HR benefits activities.

Standard Features:

- Dozens of in-depth articles on the latest news about benefits
- Benefits discussion list
- Disability forum provides case studies and in-sights into disability issues
- Current and past issues of *Employee Benefit News* available for search

www.benefitnews.com

PENSION AND WELFARE BENEFITS ADMINISTRATION

This site is provided by the U.S. Department of Labor for companies and individuals concerned with the benefit programs and mandates under the Employee Retirement Income Security Act (ERISA). Within the extended boundaries of this Web site, a dedicated reader can get an extended education on the subject and link with other complementary resources as well. Both HR professionals and typical employ-

ees can find plain language discussions of 401k programs, corporate retirement plans, industry group plans, health plans, mental health plans, plant closings, and related public policy issues.

Standard Features:

- Text of ERISA and other applicable legislation
- Text of Department of Labor regulations
- 401k program descriptions and variations
- Complete documentation of DOL activities regarding benefits administration
- Statistics on financial soundness of retirement plans
- Library of text resources
- Current news about pensions and other benefits
- DOL program descriptions
- Available as online and hard copy publication, ordering assistance
- Forms and documents

www.dol.gov/dol/pwba

SOCIAL SECURITY ONLINE

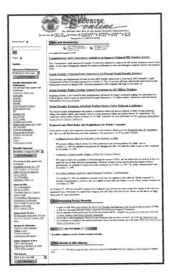

The Social Security Online Web site is the official Internet location for the Social Security Administration. Whatever you need to know, obtain, review, research, or document about Social Security can be found at this site; and there appears to be at least three different ways to find what you want as well. There is an alphabetical index down the left-hand side, a header menu, and a category/sub-category listing in the center. One of the most attractive characteristics of the site is that it can be recommended without apprehension to almost anyone who has a minimum level of comfort with Internet browsing. Hard copy publications of the Social Security Administration can be ordered online and data on personal accounts can be downloaded as well. It is an attractive, well-organized site.

Standard Features:

- Search engine
- Extensive library
- Multiple indexing modes
- Publication ordering
- Policy and procedural guidelines

www.ssa.gov

2

GENERAL INTERNET SITES

These sites are much broader than the profession of human resources, but they contain useful tools and valuable insights that can help maintain excellent linkages to the broader world and serve as resources for specific data as well. They have less of a consistent theme and more of a universal utility. Some of them you may use daily and others once a quarter, but the knowledge and flexibility they provide deserve a thorough review in order to be prepared to harness their resources when they are needed. This select group is for the human resource professionals who see their work as a career and a vocation, the kind of job that makes one look forward to Mondays.

CENTER FOR CREATIVE LEADERSHIP

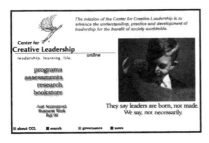

The Center for Creative Leadership was created 30 years ago and today stands as one of the largest institutions in the world committed to the understanding, practice, and development of leadership. With major campuses in Brussels, Greensboro, San Diego, and Colorado Springs, the Center conducts leadership programs, provides assessment tools & simulations to organizations, and conducts ongoing research and publishes information. The Web site contains important information about their course offerings, current research programs, and available books and materials. This is a great organization that we highly recommend to our fellow HR professionals. Give them a look!

Standard Features:

- Online Bookstore provides publications and assessment materials
- Online 360 degree feedback assessments available
- Course catalog with dates available online

www.ccl.org

CNET.COM

CNET is one of the sites HR professionals should be aware of to keep up with the trends and happenings in the technology arena. This site is a treasure trove of information: visit the help center and learn about how to better use your PC, software, even your VCR; read reviews on software and hardware; download free software; get the latest in technology news; even follow the stock market! CNET has it all for both the novice to expert technology student. Give it a look!

Standard Features:

- Reviews on desktops, notebooks, monitors, software, etc.
- Up to the minute news on technology related issues
- Financial news with a focus on technology related companies
- News & links to important Internet related tools & software
- Comparison pricing on various computer equipment
- Online auction of computer equipment
- Technology jobs database hosted by CareerBuilder
- Eye pleasing, easy to read site that is packed with information

www.cnet.com

DILBERT.COM

Every human resource professional needs an occasional break and what could be better than discovering that Catbert has been stealing your best lines. The best test of any new human resources initiative should be to check the archives of Dilbert.com for mirrored versions of the new plan. Too often, the most enlightened project is marred by a faulty execution, or the splendid cost cutting process of ten years ago has become blatantly ineffective and painfully insulting in the light of current business practices and technology. We need to examine our goals and procedures in the light of the people who are making the company real money every day, and a quick introspective look at the Dilbert Web site can help us through that process.

Standard Features:

- Current comics
- The Dilbert Store
- Last month's comics with calendar
- FAQ
- Newsletter

www.dilbert.com

FAST COMPANY

The Fast Company Web site, like its hard copy version that the site promotes, is as exhilarating as you can get sitting down and without breaking any laws. With the thought provoking articles and strong technology emphasis, it quickly becomes obvious that the editors and writers and Web masters are targeting the early adopters and cultural rebels in our society. If a human resource professional has some oversight of staffing IT jobs, or would just

like to keep up-to-date—if not slightly ahead of—current trends, both the Web site and the magazine have obvious utility. The Fast Company team wants to anticipate if not lead the charge into the new millennium. There is an incisive emphasis on the businesses, the leaders, and the ideas that will make a difference in the future. If they fall short of writing "the handbook of the business revolution," it will not be for lack of trying.

Standard Features:

- Excellent articles on business issues
- A "Net Company" presentation of ideas
- An articles index of the hard copy magazine
- An innovative approach to career management and support technologies
- Favorite bookmarks of modern managers and writers
- More good links than you can probably ever use
- Editors' manifesto

www.fastcompany.com

LYCOS

The Lycos Web site is a favorite for many human resource recruiters because it is a portal for so many of the popular job sites. Not only can you venture wherever your current search takes you, but you can quickly compare and evaluate job site performance issues for a specific open position. The collection of commercial job sites is the who's who of the industry. There are a few "also rans" and a lot of corporations that are eager enough for new talent to link themselves to Lycos. It is also useful for collecting business intelligence, keeping up with current trends in the national culture, or just satisfying human curiosity. The jobs section has a job search bookstore, a human resource section, and general career materials.

Standard Features:

- Broad collection of job sites
- Human resource section
- Job search bookstore
- Career materials
- News, health, sports, science & technology, culture
- All the miscellaneous resources typical of a general interest Internet portal

www.lycos.com

INTERNET.COM

Internet.com is simply a Web site that enables concerned users to keep up with all developments related to the Internet. HR staff may or may not need to keep their fingers on that electronic pulse, but if they do, this site will tell them more than they want to know, and allow them to be selective about their inquiries. The channels at this site can envelop you in the prices of Internet stocks, the legal implications of Internet use, the technology innovations that make it happen, the innovators who engineer its continued success, and the software you can use to get further involved.

Standard Features:

- Current Internet news
- Current Internet technology
- Web development progress
- ISP resources available
- Internet stocks information
- Internet marketing, from e-coupons to e-trading
- A download channel that puts software at your fingertips
- A collection of general Internet resources
- An international channel to help you contact overseas versions of the Web page

www.internet.com

MAMMA

With the exception of the Dr. Koop section on health, this Internet supermarket site has little direct bearing on human resources. It does contain an excellent search engine that simultaneously query's 10 other leading Internet search engines. That is why Mamma bills itself as "the mother of all search engines."

Standard Features:

- Dr. Koop on health

- White pages/yellow pages

- Reverse lookups for telephone numbers, email addresses, regular addresses, area codes, etc.

- Business search engine

- Public record searches

- Shops for gambling, mortgages, bouquets, insurance, jokes, etc.

- Job search facility that checks major sites, major newspapers, etc. and provides job search advice; a good place for HR pros to keep up with the job market

- Directory and links to career and job sites; newsgroups; a portal to almost everything in the field

- Shopping and coupons

- URL submit service

- The stock market

- Weather

- Multiple opportunities to partner with Mamma

www.mamma.com

NORTHERN LIGHT

There are several Internet search engines that you already know about—and one that you might not. Northern Light is an excellent search engine and it is by far our favorite. Northern Light is different in that it searches information from both the World Wide Web and from 5,400 premium sources. Your search now has access to millions of Web pages plus access to books, magazines, databases, and newswires 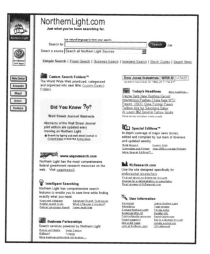 not available from any other search engine. Another key feature of the site is that results are categorized by best match and organized into topics. We highly suggest you bookmark this important Web resource.

Standard Features:

- Keyword search World Wide Web resources and premium sites with access to books, magazines, databases, and newswires and newspapers
- Premium features viewed on a pay per view basis
- Search results categorized into folders
- Advanced search capability enables user to search by dozens of predefined criteria

www.northernlight.com

WASHINGTON POST.COM

The Washington Post is one of the top newspapers in the country. Their online edition of the newspaper continues the excellence found in the print edition. Their pages are filled with up to the minute news, commentaries from top pundits, and advice from leading experts on subjects ranging from cooking to travel to employment. The utility of the Washington Post to HR professionals is twofold. On one hand, Washingtonpost.com is one of the best sites to visit to review up to the minute developments and gain in-depth context on national and worldwide events. On the other hand they have an excellent employment section where they provide a regional job board, offer advice from leading career columnists, and even host online chat sessions.

Standard Features:

- National and worldwide news updated hourly
- Site features full breadth of content from tabloid edition
- Job database and resume board with focus on the DC area
- Online chat sessions hosted daily
- Advice and commentary offered by leading career & employment experts

www.washingtonpost.com

ZD NET

ZD Net is one of the few tech-
nology-related sites we have included in the HR Top 100. As a
profession, HR has never been at
the forefront of technology issues. Our intent in including sites
such as ZD Net is to provide our
fellow colleagues with the basic
information needed to stay
abreast of technology related happenings. ZD Net is an excellent
technology related site. Ziff-
Davis or ZD is the publisher of
such notable magazines as PC Magazine, PC Week, Computer
Shopper, and Yahoo! Internet Life, etc. Contained on the ZD
Net site is much of the information found in their print publication. You can find reviews, software downloads, late breaking
technology news, and even a technology related career center.

Standard Features:

- Reviews on hardware, software, and technology related
  products
- Download Center provides access to thousands of soft-
  ware programs
- Full site search capability
- Career center featuring technology related occupations

3

HR Tools Internet Sites

When a HR professional is faced with a quick turnaround, high priority task, this collection of HR Tools is a bulwark. The sites tell you where to find that assessment tool, how to order the new book you need, where to find those ugly statistics you need for a report, and the many other resources. Here you will find the stuff that could be incredibly hard to find if this selection of sites and their descriptions were not close at hand. When you know exactly what you want and can recognize it when you find it, one of these sites probably has the answers you are looking for.

The sites are not appropriate for the green horn or the naïve; if you don't know a lot about human resources and understand most of what you know, most of these sites will be more overwhelming than helpful. You don't need a master's degree in the field, or a 30-year membership in SHRM, but neither would hurt.

BUREAU OF LABOR STATISTICS

This US government site is overflowing with data collected at taxpayer expense and so involved that it merits a thorough review by any HR professional who might need some of the key statistics found at this web site or related ones. You can find reliable data with well-designed graphs to illustrate the facts and broad insights from government professionals. Site contains excellent national and regional material for HR policy decisions.

Standard Features:

- Search function for finding data on BLS site pages
- Links to other resources
- Current news updates on labor issues
- In depth discussion of BLS services and objectives
- Listing of useful publications and research papers from government sources
- Summaries of national economic news
- Regional data with detailed specifics on labor cost trends and other material
- Surveys and programs of BLS described
- A well-designed function for user feedback

---

www.stats.bls.gov

DOW JONES INTERACTIVE

Dow Jones Interactive is a business intelligence and general data site. It harnesses for the privileged select subscribers the information gathering resources of the company that publishes the Wall Street Journal. But the site maintains a database that includes business news and views from other major newspapers as well with an 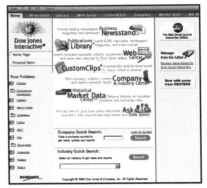 almost encyclopedic reach and a thorough indexing system. Business data on companies, their management, and their industry can be found through the site, but the quantity of free information is strictly limited. Human resource professionals should review the broad scope of information needs of their companies with multiple applications in mind. It has obvious value for marketing departments, personnel recruiting, and business strategy developers, but more extensive applications may help justify the cost for corporate participants. Dow Jones Interactive is a premier portal for business data.

Standard Features:

- Access articles and information from over 5000 newspapers, journals, periodicals, and newswires
- Mailboxes gather articles on a daily basis based on predefined user criteria
- One of the most powerful sites with tons of information—but pricey—and worth it!

www.djinteractive.com

EMPLOYEE ASSISTANCE PROFESSIONALS ASSOCIATION

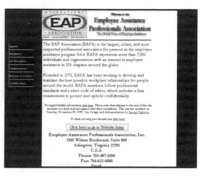

This site is a valuable guide to Employee Assistance Programs and identifies providers of related services. There is less information available on the site about EAP's than most human resource professionals would prefer, but a small, select set of links is provided and a brief text make a case for the widespread use of EAP's. Most of the site is devoted to certification, EAP provider lists, CEAP certification, conferences and other events, and a job bank for members of the association. The EAP site does not exhaust useful information on those programs, but it is a necessary reference for anything but a casual definition of this expanding human resource benefit.

Standard Features:

- Job bank
- Membership application
- Product book store
- Conference and events schedules
- Links to other related web pages
- Certification standards and process descriptions
- EAP provider lists

www.eap-association.com

HR DIRECT

The HR Direct site is simply a shopping mall for human resource professionals. Books, software, personnel forms, posters, and almost anything else that is specific to HR functions are carried through this site or its hard copy catalog. The site includes a search engine to assist shoppers in making quick and accurate purchase decisions. In addition to prompt deliveries, the site sponsor sends a level of comfort that comes from performing the necessary research to ensure that each product is functionally and legally appropriate for the intended application.

Standard Features:

- Catalog with 1200 items for HR professionals
- Search engine for finding what is needed
- Links to other web sites
- Safety posters

www.hrdirect.com

HR TOOLS

The HR Tools web site is a production of KnowledgePoint, a vendor of HR software and publications. The location displays their wares and provides links to complementary products and services, with the intent of covering a broad spectrum of human resource requirements for outside support. The organization of the site is based on a menu of HR tasks that the user can check to obtain necessary "tools" to accomplish those tasks. A toolbox concept is substituted for the traditional shopping cart we find on many commercial sites and the quantity of tools provides considerable flexibility for the HR professional using the site.

Standard Features:

- Employee screening tools
- Relocation tools
- Recruiting tools
- Training tools
- Benefits and compensation tools
- Personnel policy tools
- Performance management tools
- A convenient set of links for the Start Up table of user computers
- A collection of model job descriptions, tested for regulatory compliance
- A forms portfolio [free]
- An exemptions tester for overtime pay

www.hrtools.com

HR-ESOURCE

The HR-esource web site is a general purpose, human resource reference with an emphasis on employment law. One of the most attractive characteristics of HR-esource is the practice of enhancing its well-written and technically informed articles with cross-references to related articles [by title, source, and date]. In some cases, the article is a brief overview with the complete details available one mouse click away. Beyond a certain point, however, the site legitimately asks for a financial commitment to one of their target products, either web based or hard copy. In addition to thorough coverage, the selection of topics indicates a strong sensitivity to the issues likely to be found on a HR professional's desk for action.

Features include:

- Web products:
  International HR Advisor
  HR Advisor
  EEO Advisor
  Compensation and Benefits Advisor
  HR Wire
  HR Performance Suite (a combination of the four above)
- Product catalog
- Excellent articles on compensation & benefits
- HR related press releases nationwide
- Special reports in files to download
- Free email alerts

www.hr-esource.com

HR ONLINE

The HR Online electronic library is more of a bookstore than a library, but it has a copious selection and extensive links to other resources as well. The  amount of free useful data could be compared to the little stand of free local, ad supported magazines between the checkout clerks and the front door of a Barnes & Noble bookstore. However, the volume of contents is sufficient to justify a routine review of the resources there.

Standard Features:

- 401K resource listing
- Best Practices resource
- Compensation and benefits
- EEO and ADA employment
- Training and Development
- Software for HR solutions
- Assessment tools
- Discussion board for HR professionals on various topics
- Online surveys

www.hr2000.com

INTERNET TRAVEL NETWORK

How often have you found your-self on the phone discussing travel plans with a candidate, or needing to find the best available flights for yourself to attend a last minute meeting? Internet Travel Network provides up to date flight information along with car and hotel rentals. It is a valuable resource to have available on your desktop.

Standard Features:

- Flight schedules for all major airlines online
- Able to book reservations for flights, hotels, and cars online
- Can check the status of flights online
- "Low Fare Tickers" lists airfare deals from 25 major US cities to destinations worldwide
- Links to other important travel related resources

www.itn.com

KIERSEY TEMPERAMENT SORTER

This site contains most of what you would ever want to know about Kiersey's Temperament Sorter and Temperament Theory, a distinctive concept of human personality. There are practical applications as well as lucid descriptions of the approaches. The site is well designed and the home page is an interesting and extensive list of all the available material on the site—free and fee. The web page is a good profile of this alternative to the Myers-Briggs and Five Factor models of personality, and also has a lot of good data on child rearing. You can even take a quick questionnaire on your own temperament and character.

Standard Features:

- Resource list of books, tapes, publications, and periodicals
- Overview of theory
- Frame alternative version of site
- Links to other sources of data and insights on psychology, temperament, and personality
- Online personality assessment

www.keirsey.com

LOMINGER

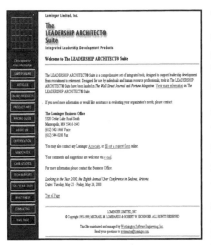

This site is also called the Leadership Suite and is sponsored by a vendor, Lominger Ltd., Inc. The LEADERSHIP ARCHITECT® Suite is a comprehensive set of integrated tools, designed to support leadership development from recruitment to retirement. In addition to marketing their software, hard copy tools, and consulting services, the site provides good articles on the kinds of heads up thinking that is leading the HR profession today. The Lominger manager team seems to have an exalted prospective on the potential contributions of HR senior management to the success of corporate America. You may not share their vision, but you should find it encouraging and challenging. This site is designed to provide professional direction and also provide some handy tools for building that future.

Standard Features:

- Articles
- Software products
- Consulting services
- Hard copy products
- Vision
- Insights

www.lominger.com

NEWSPAGE

Newspage, also known and accessed as individual.com, is an innovative site and a symbol of things to come on the Internet. In addition to obtaining an abundance of information on the site, in all the depth and variety you could ask for, the software allows the user to submit a profile or menu of the kind of news she or he wants to see on a custom basis. This site allows you to create your own news page to tell you about the issues and developments that are of immediate and regular concern to you. If this site continues to be successful, it will foster new paradigms of information collection and distribution on the Internet. HR professionals can use that kind of approach.

Standard Features:

- Headline articles
- Stock market news
- Weather news
- Computing news
- Energy news
- Mass media industry news
- General industry news
- E-commerce developments
- Your individual Internet newspaper

www.newspage.com

OUTWARD BOUND

SAME WORLD
DIFFERENT PLACE

Welcome to Outward Bound

The Outward Bound web site tells you as much about their programs as you can possibly learn without getting sweaty in the middle of one. A good review of the site will arm you to ask intelligent questions, point out valuable criteria, and even facilitate corporate involvement with Outward Bound the next time a senior executive suggests their programs as a panacea for all that ails your organization. The organization seldom fails to deliver, but the results can fail to meet expectations when companies fail to make the kind of preparations necessary for success. A human resources professional will usually have that responsibility, either explicitly or implicitly.

Standard Features:

- Course selection, online catalog and ordering of hard copy
- Course basics
- First hand accounts from participants
- Safety issues
- Environmental stewardship
- Things to know

www.outwardbound.org

PERFORMANCE APPRAISAL

The Performance Appraisal web site is sponsored by Archer North & Associates, but the most commercial aspects are the impressions earned by the insights provided without charge. The site provides a sound introduction to this critical human resources challenge, and some hints on how to meet them. The only serious shortcoming is a set of links to other useful sites.

Standard Features:

- Introduction to Performance Appraisals
- News on the topic
- Training for performance appraisals
- Sponsor's services
- Email connection
- Online Question Service

www.performance-appraisal.com

SWITCHBOARD

The Switchboard web site is a simple and quick search utility. The most attractive feature of the site is its limited focus on finding people, topics, businesses, email, maps, and message boards. It is not a HR site in the same way that calculators are not exclusively a HR tool, but it gets the job done as a search site. There are some subsidiary services like free email, free web page development software, and an intriguing utility software product for consolidating and organizing Internet bookmarks and favorite places for one's browser.

Standard Features:

- Excellent search processes
- Sound free stuff
- Locate phone numbers of businesses and individuals easily

www.switchboard.com

Tucows

Tucows.com is simply and purely a site for the downloading of software—for sale, shareware, and freeware. Tucows has been around since 1983, which makes it one of the senior locations on the Internet. Most of the software is available for a free download and you are given time to evaluate it before a purchase is necessary. This site is not only an excellent source to download software, but also an excellent site to educate the Internet & computer neophyte about the exact types of software available. Every HR professional should peruse this site at least once and we are sure you will find some valuable resources.

Standard Features:

- Hundreds of software downloads available
- Dozens of worldwide download sites makes access fast and easy
- Most software packages available for free trial
- All software is rated via a one to five cow rating system!

www.tucows.com

U. S. Census Bureau

This constitutionally mandated function of the Department of Commerce does more than conduct detailed head counts of the population every ten years. On a much more frequent basis, they collect important business information and economic data related to the worlds of commerce and culture. The sample data they collect in the interim is the basis for a broad variety of government and business decisions. Like the BLS statistics, some discretion in exploring the volumes of information is necessary in order to focus on the specific topics that impact your HR policies. A thorough one time review will help in creating plans and schedules for sampling what the Census bureau has to offer.

Standard Features:

- News and press releases on census topics
- Profiles on how people are living, and how they are spending their incomes
- How the NAICS is replacing the SIC
- Business insights
- Geographical data including maps and demographics
- A search engine to help discover good stuff
- A catalog of both free and fee statistical products
- A jobs page for opportunities with the Census Bureau
- A window into Census Bureau purpose and operations
- Population clocks with current US and world counts

www.census.gov

4

LEGAL & REGULATORY INTERNET SITES

When a normally human resource issue becomes a legal problem, whether by mischance, mischief, or neglect, it becomes much more visible, more difficult to resolve, more expensive, and more time consuming. In a litigious society where human rights are a mantra and attorneys can detect a deep corporate pocket from the next state, the human resource department that consistently avoids legal or regulatory wrangle is either very lucky or very careful.

We have selected a modest collection of dynamically helpful web sites to help you practice safe human resources. None of the sites can justify canceling the annual retainer you pay your outside legal counsel, but at least one of the senior HR pros in your shop should be tracking the impact of law on how you work with employees to achieve great results. The pace of change brings into question many policy and procedures that haven't been reviewed since they were drafted originally. An informed perspective is the best insurance against either falling on the wrong side of side of a new precedent or having your practices become the basis for that new precedent.

AHI EMPLOYMENT LAW RESOURCE CENTER

This Alexander Hamilton Institute site covers a broad array of employment law topics with clear language and a strong management orientation. The free advice is as generous as it could be without either asking the reader direct questions or offending American Bar Association guidelines. It is an excellent starting place for both practical advice on day-to-day topics and more in depth inquiries into employment law. The site sponsor does use the site to market relevant publications, but it is tastefully done and most readers will obtain obvious benefits without a purchase. The sponsors have designed and maintained an appealing site.

Standard Features:

- Links to related sites
- Problem Solver utility
- Resource page for ordering materials
- FAQ's
- Free email news summary
- Employment law chat function
- Free reports on key topics
- A feedback function
- A "What's New" page to assist HR staff keep current on employment law issues

AMERICAN ARBITRATION ASSOCIATION

This Web site is an essential study and reference resource for HR professionals who have responsibilities for agreements of any kind that include an arbitration clause. In many disputes lacking  such provisions, arbitration is often preferable to extended judicial conflicts. This non-profit's Web site provides all the definitions, philosophy, procedures, and legal background for arbitration, mediation, and other "alternative dispute resolution" processes. One key resource is the extensive text providing model arbitration clauses and discussing the alternative versions and their applications. The obvious immediate utilization would be in employment law and labor agreements, but the delivery of health benefits and lease agreements for facilities could also be productive. While the extensive articles at the web site are not a substitute for attorney review, they do enable HR professionals to make thoughtful choices. You can find the complete text of the 1996 federal legislation that is the legal basis for alternative dispute resolution and a long list of links to organizations and associations that are references for applications in different industries.

Standard Features:

- Complete text background for the process, drafts, and definitions
- Legal basis for the processes
- Links to knowledgeable organizations
- Contact information nationwide
- Membership data
- Background on related research

www.adr.org

CORNELL UNIVERSITY LEGAL INFORMATION

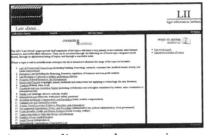

The Cornell University Legal Information Institute is an excellent resource for legal information. In addition to such HR related topics as employment law, workers compensation, and labor law, many other types of law categories are discussed—taxation, constitutional law, and family law. Each area of law has a descriptive overview, which is several paragraphs long and gives the "basics". Additionally, links to appropriate federal and state statutes and judicial decisions are presented. Links to additional references are also provided which makes this site a top launching pad to research legal information.

Standard Features:

- Links to related sites
- Full site keyword search
- Law topic overviews
- Alphabetical listing of topics

www.law.cornell.edu/topical.html

ELAWS ADVISORS

Elaws Advisors is a service of the U.S. Department of Labor. This service was created to help both employers and employees understand their rights and responsibilities under several of the laws and regulations under the DOL's jurisdiction. Each Advisor works by imitating the interaction you might have with a DOL employment law expert—it asks questions and based on your answers, narrows down to providing the appropriate response. This is an excellent source to obtain important information on DOL Laws and regulations. We suggest you add it to your bookmark list for future reference.

Standard Features:

- Easy to use interactive functionality
- Summary of laws administered by the Dept. of Labor
- Keyword and agency type search of site contents

www.dol.gov/elaws

EQUAL EMPLOYMENT OPPORTUNITY COMMISSION

This Web site is brought to us by the US Equal Employment Opportunity Commission and it contains all the data human resource professionals need to know, but would rather not digest at one sitting. A brief intellectual dive into the volumes available has potential for provoking an anxiety attack and a dark conviction that you have inadvertently violated one of the regulatory precepts cited. It will pass. If the scope of the law intimidates, the Web site text clarifies the boundaries of employment behaviors in plain, unambiguous language. To supplement the Web site resources, the EEOC offers both training and contact information for regional offices.

Standard Features:

- Definitions of EEOC coverage
- Contact information
- Brief descriptions of recent EEOC achievements and penalties
- Guidelines on the different kinds of EEOC violations
- List of training available
- Text available for downloading
- Press releases
- Administrative enforcement activities

www.eeoc.gov

EQUAL OPPORTUNITY PUBLICATIONS

The Equal Opportunity Publications site is a private enterprise endeavor that creates publications for personnel covered under the EEOC law and regulations. As an advocate to equal opportunity, EOP, Inc. also collects resumes from job seekers and distributes them to interested employers.

Standard Features:

- Resume database

- Jobs database

- Employers hiring list, with contact information

- Subscription information

- Five EEOC/diversity periodicals identified

- An IT (Information Technology) magazine recently launched

FAIR MEASURES—LEGAL TRAINING FOR MANAGERS

This Fair Measures site is sponsored by a training organization staffed by attorneys and their specialty is employment law. The site promotes a full array of training seminars, publications, films, and other materials that a HR person can order. They also provide an excellent set of links to related sites, employment law topics covered in a question and answer format, and non-legal text descriptions of important cases for the past three or four years. The quantity and quality of the information is impressive, and obvious care is taken to remain both current and accurate on legal employment issues.

Standard Features:

- Tapes, films, and books for sale
- Links to related sites
- A description of training programs available
- Employment law described in question and answer format
- Summaries of recent precedent setting cases

www.fairmeasures.com

HR LAW INDEX

The HR Law Index is a comprehensive collection of data about HR oriented legal issues, supplemented by links to other related resources. This site complements the AHI site by providing a listing of applicable court cases and administrative judgments, and a layman friendly short description of the cases and their disposition. For HR professionals who need to dig deeper, the attorneys of record and the Lexis citation are provided as a footnote to the

description. The HR Law Index also provides abundant articles by attorneys on specific employment law issues. This site is a must for both decision-making on current situations and the establishment of policies and procedures to preclude future difficulties.

Standard Features:

- Extensive lay citations on employment law issues
- Articles on employment law issues
- Model employment law policies and procedures
- Lay firm articles
- Law journal articles
- Government documents
- Selected law firms referenced
- Clear and easy contact procedures
- 24 hour free trial, $95 annual membership

www.hrlawindex.com

LAW JOURNAL EXTRA—EMPLOYMENT AND LABOR LAW

The Law Journal Extra site focuses on labor law and employment law issues, providing articles and reports on related cases in nationwide judicial decisions. It is a division or practice feature of the National Law Journal and has links to other key labor law resources. The site covers legal news and contains columns on legal issues as well, handling a broad range of employment law.

Standard Features:

- Articles on employment law issues
- News reports on recent legal or regulatory decisions
- Archives of less current but still important cases
- Links to other employment law sites

'LECTRIC LAW LIBRARY EMPLOYMENT & LABOR

This site covers the same bases as other Internet sources for human resource professionals, but with distinctions both helpful and challenging. One of the most positive features is the grouping of similar employment law cases together to minimize the amount of effort necessary to review relevant cases. Those page links also include the length of the file in thousands of bytes, indicated by a number and the letter "K." Because 2K is typically one page long, that detail gives the reader a quick estimate of how much printing would be required for a copy and how long it will take to read it online. Depending on the background of the HR person reading the files, the letter for letter copy of the legal complaint leading to a law suit will either be enlightening or a conceptual burden. The principal advantage of that approach is that the legal precedents are cited, and they are helpful in anticipating how a case may be decided.

Standard Features:

- Legal issue articles
- Law suit text
- Links to other sources
- Membership fees for in depth data
- Broad coverage with clear delineation of topics
- A law dictionary
- A law library, and selected e-text books

www.lectlaw.com

NATIONAL LABOR RELATIONS BOARD

The National Labor Relations Board site is as comprehensive as you would expect of one with almost unlimited funds to spend, that represents a federal bureaucracy, and has a 65 year history of conflicts, precedents, and policy changes to document. The main menu has fifteen options that encompass the details of the National Labor Relations Act and most of the current applications to the world of work. To help users manage what could be information overload; the site includes both a Help Desk function and a list of regional NLRB office contacts to back up the site with real people to provide guidance on related issues. The only dark spot on an otherwise excellent site is the Freedom of Information Act choice; it will, without warning or provocation, disable mouse, keyboard, and a Windows 98 operating system. The only cure is to cut off your computer, and start over.

Standard Features:

- A superb set of menu options
- Up-to-date press releases, public notices, and important decision summaries
- Detailed text documents—the enabling legislation, forms, policies, procedures, manuals, and publications
- Spanish language access
- NLRB job opportunities listings

www.nlrb.gov

OCCUPATIONAL SAFETY AND HEALTH ADMINISTRATION

Having an OSHA inspector visit your place of business is like hearing that the family car has been wrecked—you feel bad about the situation, but you are more concerned about any injuries that may have happened. The human resource professionals, who both take the time to understand this site and exercise the initiative to address the OSHA guidelines, can avoid a major part of that distress. Like other regulatory Web sites, this one is festooned with awesome amounts of information and distinct learning opportunities.

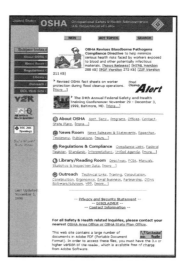

Standard Features:

- Text of the enabling legislation and documented changes to the OSHA mandate
- News summary covering all public discussion and official press releases
- Directories of staff and related contact data
- Library of useful books on safety
- Success stories
- Arrangements with state units cited

www.osha.gov

5

OD/CHANGE MANAGEMENT INTERNET SITES

How many psychologists does it take to change a light bulb?
Only one, but the light bulb must really want to change.

OD/Change Management is one of the glorious opportunities and dire quagmires facing human resource persons. Ambitious executives perceive worlds of promise in the task of changing organizations and/or people, and often have difficulty distinguishing between the two very different objectives.

Human resource professionals often find themselves with the precarious task of diplomatically explaining the distinctions and leading their managers in defining what the real potential is for their organization and in the building of programs for timely achievement. It is not an easy role, but the three sites outlined here can provide both guidance and a gateway to other online resources.

ASSOCIATION FOR QUALITY AND PARTICIPATION

The Association for Quality and Participation, is an international not-for-profit membership association. The Association is dedicated to improving workplaces through quality and participation practices. The focus of the site is on organization development, change management, and quality related issues. Expect to find articles from leading change experts on the site along with information on the Baldridge Award, seminars, and publications for purchase. HR professionals who are involved in OD practices should give this organization a look.

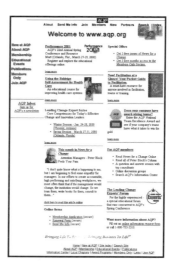

Standard Features:

- E-newsletter sent to interested participants
- Local chapters along with key contact listed
- Association seminars listed
- Online membership application

www.aqp.org

BUSINESS PROCESS REENGINEERING LEARNING CENTER

This site is sponsored by the Prosci Research and Publishing Company and is a good location for getting your feet wet on the reengineering process. The history of high hype and mixed successes make it imperative that human resource professionals be well informed whenever reengineering becomes a gleam in the eye of the CEO. As anticipated, the site has an extensive bookstore of reengineering articles and execution templates. Benchmarks by industry and job type, tutorials, best practices, surveys, and links to online articles should help avoid some of the many pitfalls, and enable change management teams to complete a reengineering project with confidence and competence. Some of the resources are expensive, but so is reengineering.

Standard Features:

- Mailing lists
- Bookstore
- Links to articles on reengineering
- Feedback to Web site sponsors
- Directory of experienced professionals
- Tutorials
- Reengineering and project management software
- Directory of training resources

www.prosci.com

ORGANIZATIONAL DEVELOPMENT NETWORK

You can find everything you need to change on this site, and a warm fuzzy feeling about the new you as well. The volunteers who maintain the site demonstrate their expertise in Web page and organizational development. There are the usual collection of event announcements, job listings, and publication sales. But the most attractive aspect of the site are the email communities of OD people who share special bonds, professional or otherwise. The best ones provide a potential for electronic collaboration for OD specialists, but the open discussion forum allows the less informed and experienced to learn more about the field quickly without getting an advanced degree. It is a good model for other professional organization Web sites.

Standard Features:

- Complete listing of coming events
- A job site for OD specialists
- Organizational updates
- Membership sign up software
- Five professional sharing email lists
- A directory of OD practitioners
- A directory of colleges and universities where OD training can be obtained in an academic setting
- Well written descriptions of the organization and its principles and practices

---

www.odnet.org

6

PROFESSIONAL INTERNET SITES

A ll of the sites in this book are professional, but a few have the special distinction of being strongly focused upon and thoroughly useful for the human resource professional. Some have a narrow scope, but they have an extraordinary value for HR managers. The topics covered are as comprehensive as the Society for Human Resource Management's site and as narrow as one describing the pros and cons of off-site and at home employee work.

These have the virtue of single-minded in their emphasis and displaying more depth of thought than one usually finds on the Internet. The data is not updated at a rapid pace and does not need to be. These are sites you can have on your computer when your boss comes by for a visit.

AMERICAN ASSOCIATION FOR AFFIRMATIVE ACTION

The American Association for Affirmative Action Web page is a strong example of a well-developed institutional description. The site does not provide all the insights and background needed for maintaining an excellent affirmative action process, but it is an excellent place to begin. In addition to abundant links to other resources, the site describes the training and communications opportunities available in this critical aspect of human resource

management. Considering the ongoing debates about the role of affirmative action in the work place, a central point for up-to-date information and developments is a valuable resource. Besides being an eager advocate of its services, the site is an excellent portal to federal records and resources as well as professional journals and regional materials.

Standard Features:

- Excellent collection of links
- Membership data
- Organizational events description and schedule
- Guidelines about the scope and practical applications of affirmative action

www.affirmativeaction.org

AMERICA ONLINE WORKPLACE

(AOL membership required) Though not technically on the Internet, the AOL workplace section is an area that HR professionals need to visit. With close to 20 million members America Online is a force in the online world. The Workplace section of AOL is quite an interesting site. You will find information on start-up businesses, a career center with links to job databases, a resume bank, online chat and message boards about career related topics, even business news and business research. Give it a look!

Standard Features:

- A full function career center with job links, career advice, career research, etc.
- Online career chat rooms
- Career message boards
- 20 million plus visitors

www.aol.com

HR NEXT

HR Next is a commercial Internet information Web site; distributing news, concepts, and experience of direct and immediate interest to human resource professionals. Software, publications, and hard copy materials are also available, and a search engine is there to help users find any resource that the site cannot provide directly. Free text articles supply general interest commentary on current topics and planning resources have potential to reduce the workload of human resource professionals.

Standard Features:

- Federal labor law posters
- HR software
- Personnel forms
- Communications tools
- Contact the Web site function

www.hrnext.com

HR PLAZA

The HR Plaza site is another general purpose HR site that cushions its product presentations with valuable information about the industry. The text covers conventions and other events, and discussions on current issues. The site is also well linked to other useful ones specializing in HR activities.

Standard Features:

- HR job site with corporate search capacity and job candidate resumes; but restricted to human resource professionals. Job listings cover a wide geographic area, but the search engine simplifies the process for both job searchers and talent seekers

- The links are divided into categories that expedite the search process

- A Career Mosaic job site

- Affiliation with Bernard Hodes, Inc.

www.hrplaza.com

HR TODAY

HR Today is a broad topic Web site with a newspaper motif of articles on various current matters. In addition there is an online bookstore and other support facilities from Weddle's, and a link to an undistinguished site for jobs and resumes. The site also provides links to a collection of human resource professionals. The feedback [guest book] opportunity is commendable and the articles are apparently updated weekly. The site is worth a place on your schedule for keeping up to date on recruiting/retention in particular and human resources in general.

Standard Features:

- Solid quality professional articles
- A job site
- The Weddle Catalog of books on recruiting and job searches
- A weekly email to remind HR pros to check out the site for new articles
- Useful links to a variety of HR professionals
- Links to college placement offices

www.jobfind.com/hrtoday

Human Resources Institute

The Human Resources Institute provides research reports, white papers, conducts surveys, and sponsors seminars and conferences on strategic human resources and people issues. It is an organization comprised of HR Professionals, Organizational Psychologists, and researchers who provide cutting edge information on issues to sponsoring organizations. Several of the reports on the site are free whereas others are available only to sponsoring organizations. Peruse the site, see if your organization is a sponsor, and consider becoming a sponsor if you find useful information. We were impressed!

Standard Features:

- Research reports, white papers, and surveys available to member organizations. Some free reports available to the general public
- Links to other HR information provided
- Site search capability
- Listing of sponsoring organizations provided

hri.eckerd.edu

Institute of Management & Administration

The Institute of Management & Administration Web site publishes a variety of information for business professionals. They cite 180,000 members and editors from a collection of leading US corporations as key features of the organization. The scope of  coverage expands beyond strictly human resource issues, but the material that does is very useful and a general familiarity with important management issues should not be a handicap for human resource professionals. There is an interesting combination of free and fee resources, and the Institute is beginning a management library Web site to supplement their current offerings.

Standard Features:

- A management library providing a broad selection of free articles and opportunities to purchase more comprehensive collection
- A Medicare knowledge resource
- A business directory
- A Law Office Management and Administrative Report (LOMAR)
- IOMA Product listing
- A complete salary survey and discussion section

www.ioma.com

INTERNATIONAL TELECOMMUTING ADVISORY COUNCIL

ITAC is a non-profit organization dedicated to promoting the economic, social, and environmental benefits of teleworking. Members share information about the design and implementation of teleworking programs, the development of the U.S. telework sector, and research. ITAC is a Washington based organization with supporting heavy hitters in the industry and government. The organization cites impressive statistics in improved productivity and a survey indicating 10% of the current US workforce are telecommuters. If telecommuting has potential for your company, this site provides techniques to evaluate its overall feasibility, and if implemented, ways to minimize the risks and pitfalls.

Standard Features:

- Recent press releases on the topic of telecommuting
- A complete series of online workshops
- Development of best practices progress reports
- Reporting on legislative support for telecommuting
- Conference planning, schedules, and registration
- Teleconference opportunities
- Membership subscription
- Buyers guide to products and services
- Telework library

www.telecommute.org

JOB ACCOMMODATION NETWORK

The Job Accommodation Network (JAN) provides technical support and assistance for both people with disabilities and to businesses on how to fashion job site accommodations. JAN was founded by the President's Committee on Employment of People with Disabilities and is located at West Virginia University. The JAN Web site provides all the pertinent information needed by businesses and HR professionals regarding the Americans with Disabilities Act.

Standard Features:

- Complete list of documents about ADA issues
- Links to other ADA related sites
- Complete summary of the ADA provided

janweb.icdi.wvu.edu

LABOR ONLINE

Labor Online is a look into the heart of the labor movement. Please don't be distracted by the page that quotes rates for helping union organizations develop their own Web pages. The "links" page is your source for insights into the history, perspectives, issues, and philosophy of organized labor in the United States. Some vacant links mar the utility of an otherwise excellent Web site. If your company has a bargaining unit, or there is a possibility of one developing, you should survey this site on a regular basis.

Standard Features:

- Feedback opportunities
- A collection of links to key labor sites
- The text of favorite union songs
- The "Don't Buy" boycott list
- Important labor quotes

www.laboronline.com

SOCIETY FOR HUMAN RESOURCE MANAGEMENT

The SHRM site is the Web portal for the human resource profession. All the good things that the Society for Human Resource Management does for its membership and the larger human resource community is represented here, setting a high standard for other career organizations desiring a presence on the Internet. One can use the site to find an HR job, track legislative progress of workplace oriented legislation, catch a vision of where the profession is going, order materials from the bookstore, find a good HR consultant, make career choices, and link to another Internet resource on almost any related topic. The site is so good that SHRM must limit some of its features to members only. You can join online as well, but you can get the value of an annual membership just perusing the free stuff on this Web site.

Standard Features:

- Articles on a broad range of HR topics
- Membership sign up
- Bookstore
- HR news
- Professional insights

www.shrm.org

SOCIETY FOR INDUSTRIAL/ORGANIZATIONAL PSYCHOLOGY

The SIOP site is a home base for anyone who is excited about I-O psychology, and all HR pros should become familiar with the basics of the practice. You can find those basics here. Useful text resources not printed out in the site can be downloaded easily. In addition to providing an open-ended introduction to the field, the site is a good coordinator for the membership. A search engine facilitates finding the email addresses of members and a current salary survey keeps them up-to-date on compensation issues. The bookstore contains publications and T-shirts.

Standard Features:

- Membership information
- Bookstore
- Professional background information
- Conference information

Work Index

Workindex.com is produced by the publishers of Human Resource Executive magazine, in co-operation with Cornell University's School of Industrial Labor Relations. The index will prove invaluable to anyone looking for workplace information, including corporate HR professionals, top executives, line managers and job seekers around the world. Those interested in human resources, labor relations, benefits, training, technology, staffing, recruiting, leadership, motivation, insurance, relocation, legal issues and more, will make use of this valuable tool.

Standard Features:

- HR News
- Legal Clinic
- Job Posting
- Online book store
- Ten selected Web sites of special interest to HR professionals; changed frequently
- HR software with free test drives for evaluation

www.workindex.com

WORKFORCE ONLINE

Workforce Online is a Web site best described as human resources with an attitude. The editors express commitment to the concept of HR professionals being valued and dynamic contributors to the top level management decisions, as having real impact in the organizations that they serve. Their vision is reflected in their ten book reading list, the HR News captured on the site, links to other HR sites, a proactive legal clinic, the selection of HR software sold, and a job site that is mirrored in a series of excellent sites.

Standard Features:

- Bookstore and reading list
- Extensive links to other quality HR sites
- HR news column with links
- A legal clinic that covers current issues
- Good selection of HR software
- Job site with fee for resume review, but no charges for placing ads

www.workforceonline.com

7

RECRUITING INTERNET SITES

While you will find lots of useful information by reading our book on Internet recruiting, *The Employers' Guide to Recruiting on the Internet,* you will also find several excellent online recruitment resources. This chapter highlights the major sites that leading firms use in their Internet based recruiting efforts and also includes some sites that must be studied in order to understand what the Internet has done to the process of recruiting and retaining outstanding employees.

A careful exploration should help human resource professionals select those job sites that will be most productive and cost effective for their companies, and also help them to view the process from the job candidate's perspective.

The big corporate winners in the next decade will be the talent-powered companies who consciously and deliberately incorporate hiring and motivating superior talent as a strategic policy. Many of them already have a two to three year head start on the competitors in their industry. These sites don't contain all the insights you need, but they go a long way in assisting you with the process.

AMERICAS JOB BANK

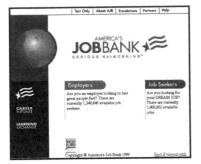

Americas Job Bank is the job site sponsored by all the Employment Security operations in the United States. The distinctive advantage is the low cost to employers and job seekers, and the broad coverage. Theoretically, all companies with any kind of federal business are required to list their jobs on this site, and the unemployed place their resumes here. The site is often overwhelmed by the quantity of job ads inserted there by headhunters who want to minimize their advertising expenses, but companies can get a lot of bang for their buck here and possibly dodge some of those headhunter fees. The site typically has over 1 million job seekers, not to mention a similar number of jobs.

Standard Features:

- Large quantity of job candidates
- Economic job postings
- Extensive listing of career education and training resources
- Extensive listing of career planning assistance available from government sources

www.ajb.dni.us

CAREER BUILDER NETWORK

Career Builder is considered a top ten Internet job board. Like several of the other job boards, they have thousands of ads in a searchable database where individuals can search by location, employment type, and keyword. Unlike other job boards they have a few interesting features. The most outstanding feature is the network concept. Instead of being one single job board, CareerBuilder is a network of 25+ boards. Employers choose

which board or boards they desire to advertise on. Another feature that is novel is the mega-search capability of their search engine. Job seekers can search not only the 25+ CareerBuilder network job boards, but also other major sites such as Monster.com, Americas Job Bank, Job Options, etc.

Standard Features:

- Keyword searchable employment ad database
- Career News from USA Today
- Links to Web based career articles and resources
- Directory of employers advertising on the site
- Free email boxes to job seekers
- Emailing of matching jobs to job seekers

www.careerbuilder.com

CAREERMOSAIC

CareerMosaic is one of the pioneering commercial job sites and still maintains a strong commitment to excellent service. In addition to a diverse listing of job search communities that group all of the ads and resumes into easily distinguished patterns, CareerMosaic provides an extended selection of resources for the job seeker. There is an employer user charge of approximately $100 per month for resume searches. The chief attraction of this site is the quantity and quality of job candidates. For employers with large and persistent staff needs, both the resume search and job ads can be a bargain.

Standard Features:

- Free resume posting
- Paid job ads
- Paid resume access
- Effective search interface
- Advice to job seekers

www.careermosaic.com

CAREERPATH

CareerPath is a great job site for companies unwilling to wean themselves from the traditional newspaper help wanted ad, and with a timid approach to technological innovation. CareerPath is the Internet job site where a collection of large and small newspapers place the job ads published in their hard copy periodical on the information highway as well. It is not a bad deal if you must print an ad in the newspaper anyway, but what you say in the newspaper ad is exactly what you get in the CareerPath Internet ad.

Standard Features:

- General career advice for job seekers
- A broad distribution of jobs nationwide
- Functional search engine
- Chat rooms
- Company profiles
- Nearly 90 newspapers represented
- Online job posting for speed and convenience
- Automatic posting
- Job fairs

www.careerpath.com

CAREERS.WSJ.COM

This site is sponsored by the Wall Street Journal, and in this site they make a direct pitch to the employer and employee elite in the labor marketplace. They have diligently included all the features that you could imagine for an Internet job site, and still be tasteful and proper. The Wall Street Journal has drawn from an eminent stable of writers to present high quality articles about careers and have constructed a site that can be navigated by the less computer literate as well. Companies with specialized needs for talent should check this site for similar jobs and consider advertising here if it obviously attracts the type of person for whom they are searching.

Standard Features:

- Jobs listings
- Resume listings
- Bookstore
- Job search and career advice
- Advice on salaries, profits
- A directory of who is hiring
- Industry trends in employment
- Serious research on salaries
- Excellent articles on national and regional trends

www.careers.wsj.com

ComputerJobs.com

The ComputerJobs.com Web site is exactly what you would expect from the title, a job site completely dedicated to advertising jobs for and containing the resumes of Information Technology personnel. The search process for career seekers begins with a geographic preference and narrows down to areas of demonstrated expertise. It is an aggressive marketplace of scarce engineering and programming talent, and the competitive flavor is enhanced by Web managers who promise hourly updates to both the jobs and the resume databases. ComputerJobs.com provides its visitors with a wealth of resources, including interactive message boards, training resources, user group listings, access to IT-related discussion groups, technical publication links, and its own dynamic salary survey. The site was awarded the number one ranking in three out of six categories in the 1999 Electronic Recruiting Index including Customer Satisfaction, Results Quality, and Long-Term Growth/Investment Potential.

Standard Features:

- Smoothly operating job and resume databases
- Free resume submission
- Over 32,000 IT jobs
- Message boards
- Training resources
- Salary surveys

www.computerjobs.com

DISCOVERME.COM

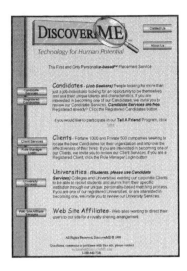

The DiscoverMe.com Web site is an employment matching site with a unique approach. Instead of a resume dependent, skills based evaluation process, job candidates register with the site and complete a personality traits assessment free of charge. The client companies also register and submit a personality profile that fits the people who have been most successful in the open position. Then the DiscoverMe.com software performs a matching process, and advises the job candidates that fit of the possible corporate interest in their potential. They decide whether to make the contact and begin the exchange of information that may lead to a job offer. This approach can work for soft skills, not the Oracle systems administrators with ten years of experience. For companies who perform extensive in house training and hire based on key interpersonal characteristics, this technique could be productive. The application of this process to recent college graduates in liberal arts is obvious.

Standard Features:

- Job candidate registration and assessment
- Client recruiter registration

www.discoverme.com

ELECTRONIC RECRUITING EXCHANGE

The Electronic Recruiting Exchange is a portal to learning about the electronic recruiting process. Using the ERE directory, you can access several recruiting based forums, a job site for recruiter job candidates, consultants, job boards, publications, recruiter support, assessment technology, salary surveys, search firms, recruiting software, and recruiter training events. This site does not have the best resources in every category, but

the full deck of choices and recruiter focus make this an obvious early location to check for recruiting answers. The forums are a special favorite for an impressive collection of corporate recruiters as well as headhunters. Most of the resources are free and the return on investment for one's time is attractive.

Special Features:

- A recruiter discussion list keeps you up to date on happenings in the staffing industry
- Recruiter bookstore
- Recruiter job bank
- Recruiting industry news

www.erexchange.com

Headhunter.net

The Headhunter.net site has over 200,000 resumes and 160,000 jobs posted and the specific feature that distinguishes it from many other sites is the ability of both job seekers and companies to exercise some control about how their data—job ads and resumes—appear on the Internet. The anonymity this offers currently employed, passive job seekers makes its particularly attractive to them. For employers, the site provides the capacity to move a given job ad to the top of those in its category—for a fee. The site is a rich repository of computer related jobs, but also connects a significant number of engineering, accounting/financial, and sales/marketing jobs.

Standard Features:

- Smoothly functioning database of jobs and job seekers
- Well-designed user interface
- Easy to read, clear organization of data
- A fee schedule that allows user to buy premium positioning
- Anonymous resume posting
- Disciplined removal of stale resumes
- Good feedback function
- Password access for job seekers and employers
- Clear standards for users

www.headhunter.net

HOT JOBS

Hot Jobs is another Internet job site. The special feature that distinguishes it is the capability of jobseekers to review the list of companies with access to the site and block their current employer from viewing their resume. This makes it, like Headhunter.net, a particularly attractive site for passive job seekers who chose  not to upset current employers. For employers, there is an increased likelihood that the resume they like represents someone who has a job. Also, this site endeavors to exclude headhunter job ads, allowing companies to compete with each other instead of vendors for talented job seekers.

Standard Features:

- Excellent database search processes
- Good job listing procedures
- Company profiles provide superb employer exposure
- Personal search statistics, message boards, free email, personal search agents, and company block functions attract serious job seekers
- Site provides an applicant tracking and Web-recruiting management software
- Banner ads and competitive pricing available to companies
- High quality site design

www.hotjobs.com

JOB OPTIONS

Job Options is an Internet job site with a twist. This venerable site was once called Espan and earned a significant following before it changed through AdNet to JobOptions. With over 6000 corporate clients using it to find good candidates, the job candidates find Job Options attractive.
Additional features allow the job seeker to remain anonymous by utilizing a combination of search agents and blind resumes. The search agent compares the candidates choice of search text to use in reviewing its thousands of current jobs on file and advises the job candidate by email of those that are a preliminary fit. The candidate can also file a blind resume, and when a company expresses an interest to Job Options, Job Options tells the candidate about the company job and allows him or her to decide whether or not to make contact with the prospective employer. There is also a separate database of open resumes for the review of serious corporate employers.

Standard Features:

- Job filings for a fee
- Resume filings free
- Search engines to connect the parties to each other
- More control available for the job candidate
- Three options for job candidates—open resumes, blind resumes, and key word search of the job database
- Good Web site controls

www.joboptions.com

JOB TRAK

Job Trak is the major site for recent [and future] college graduates and alumni who keep in touch with their placement office to discover new opportunities. It is a straightforward Web site with good Web skills displayed throughout. HR staffs should find excellent candidates with entry level ambitions, and it will  be easy enough to specify the college or university from which you hope and plan to recruit.

Standard Features:

- Jobs database
- Resume database
- Registration processes
- Links to other resources
- Easy edits of contact information
- High interest from employers

www.jobtrak.com

MONSTER.COM

The Monster has spared no expense in either developing or promoting its monster sized and extended coverage job site. It currently contains over 250,000 jobs and an electronic ton of resumes. The Monster site contains a broad collection of services for both employers and job candidates. The ambitious reach covers jobs from fresh out of school graduates to senior executives and high tech computer professionals. The exhaustive choices for both employers and potential employees are made less taxing by excellent search process software. Contract employees and international jobs are included.

Standard Features:

- Large database of jobs, but awkward to use
- Large database of resumes
- Advice for job seekers
- Company research database
- Career centers for different categories of job seekers
- Banner ads and other employer recruiting enhancements
- Chat rooms for job seekers
- Newsletter
- Message boards
- Automated resume submission

www.monster.com

NATIONAL ASSOCIATION OF COLLEGES AND EMPLOYERS

This job site is designed especially for the new college graduate. The National Association of Colleges and Employers is a joint effort of large corporate employers and those human resource professionals known as college placement staff. The Web site is designed to complement and supplement 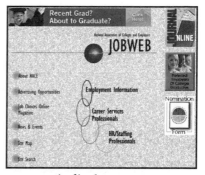 their extensive collection of hard copy periodicals on career management for alumni as well as recent graduates. But they have not been reluctant to include valuable data and opportunities on the Web site itself. The sound and ethical approach to the placement mission may earn this site a growing share of the total job ad industry.

Standard Features:

- Well-designed jobs database
- High quality resume database
- Excellent corporate profiles
- Excellent research into employment issues
- Career fairs
- Catalogs
- News and event listings for job seekers, HR professionals, and media interests

www.jobweb.org

RECRUITER RESOURCES

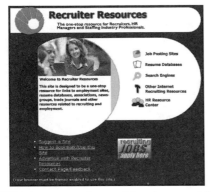

The Recruiter Resources Web page is designed to be the one stop location for recruiters of all types and objectives. While that may be too large a challenge, Recruiter Resources is a sound attempt. With links to over 250 job site links, over 120 resume sites, over 90 search engines, over 200 general recruiting sites, and 80 HR interest sites, this site establishes itself as a highly useful portal to the work of finding good job candidates. The Web page structure is elegant and the links are grouped for quick referencing to the type of site you need.

Standard Features:

- Links to job sites
- Links to resume sites
- Links to search engines
- Links to general recruiting sites
- Links to HR professional resources
- Help in book marking the site with major browsers
- Straightforward feedback function

www.recruiterresources.com

RECRUITERS NETWORK

The Recruiters Network site provides both a system of directories of recruiting links and Web pages with insights on how to use them effectively. The job site it directly sponsors is one for HR professionals, but it links to the other major sites as well. The various services are both free and useful with financial support coming from banner ads and sales of software and publications. The Web page articles touch on almost every imaginable recruiting issue and are consistently well written. A listserv provides a communications vehicle for exchanging ideas and information with other Internet recruiting professionals.

Standard Features:

- Job site for HR professionals
- Links to other sites
- Good articles on recruiting and related topics
- Shopping list of software and training available; serves as shopping portal
- List of sponsors
- Free membership
- Assortment of discounts on products and services

www.recruitersnetwork.com

RECRUITERS ONLINE NETWORK

The Recruiters Online Network is a job site designed by headhunters for headhunters, but it deserves a good inspection because of the quantity of jobs and resumes there. There are thousands of jobs and approximately 8,000 third party recruiters (headhunters) using the site. The site caters to that specialized market, but a review of the jobs available should provide useful insights into the current labor market for the positions that you need to fill and the sources of corporate turnover, if that is a problem. The site is well designed and maintained, and if you really need a third party recruiter, there is an extensive directory organized by type and region. "A global community of recruiters, headhunters, and professional staffing firms."

Standard Features:

- Resume database (available for headhunter members only)
- Jobs database
- Directory of headhunters

www.ipa.com

RILEY GUIDE

The Riley Guide is a job candidate oriented portal to the job search process, providing Internet links, job search articles, shortcuts and hints, resume examples, and other resources. Of special interest to the human resource recruiter, there are links to and descriptions of a comprehensive selection of salary survey Web pages. Any review of current salary ranges and compensation policies should review relevant material on this site in addition to conducting appropriate local research. The most helpful aspect of this Web page will be the opportunity to look at the labor market from the other side of the desk that often separates interviewer from interviewee. In addition to the large list of job sites listed, the Riley Guide also provides a brief overview and general evaluation.

Standard Features:

- Job site list
- Job search articles
- Copious salary survey data
- Salary negotiation articles

www.dbm.com/jobguide

VAULT.COM

Vault.com has developed into quite an interesting career board in recent years. Made famous by publishing hundreds of employer profiles for potential employees, they have switched their concentration to focus on being a full service workplace network. In addition to the reports that made them famous you will also find company message boards where thousands of individuals discuss what they like and hate about their current employer. Additionally the site contains such features as job listings, career newsletters, a bookstore, and company research. This site represents the enormous potential of the Internet to disseminate information. In this case it is information about your organization to potential employees. HR professionals need to take notice of this in light of our new talent driven marketplace.

Standard Features:

- Online reports of hundreds of American corporations
- Message boards with thousands of comments about employment at various organizations
- Over 100,000 jobs online from 20,000+ employers
- Job listings matched and emailed to job seekers
- Over one dozen targeted career newsletters emailed to job seekers weekly

www.vaultreports.com

8

RELOCATION INTERNET SITES

O
ften a necessary corollary to recruitment and frequently
involved in related responsibilities, managing someone's
relocation is one of the necessary ordeals of many human resource careers. Well-managed relocations can be evidence
of how well the company or organization values the past, present,
and future contributions of new hires and the corporate heroes
needed somewhere else. On the other hand, a less than smooth
transition can be a source of stress that detracts from productivity
and does real damage to staff retention.

The sites selected provide a choice between outsourcing the
process and simply finding utilitarian resources to share some of
the burden of managing the transition. The choice depends greatly
on the volume of relocations to be handled and the access to appropriate resources. The sites cover all of the aspects of relocation
except how to translate your HR successes in this area into a big
promotion and appropriate raise.

HOMEFAIR

Homefair is a consumer oriented collection of utilities for individuals, but is a valuable tool for HR professionals to introduce to prospects, new hires, and employees for the management of issues regarding relocation, home buying, insurance, and a multitude of other personal matters. The site is an excellent and independent third party resource that an Internet equipped person who wants to investigate the issue without undue reliance on the patience and background of their contacts in human resources should find useful.

Standard Features:

- Plan a move—truck rentals, movers
- Plan a home purchase, calculate mortgage payments, fees, etc.
- Schedule a relocation, research locations, investigate sites
- Rent an apartment
- Cost of living comparisons
- Good checklists for decision making
- School evaluations
- General consumer advice
- Address labels for the move

www.homefair.com

MORTGAGE NET

The Mortgage Net is the next best thing to having a devoted father in the real estate business. This site aspires to provide all the insights and services one needs to buy a home and to the best of our knowledge, covers all the bases. The focus is on the financing of a new residence, of course, but all aspects are investigated— finding; evaluating; selecting features;  deciding between existing homes or contracting with a builder; finding a broker, contractor, or repair specialist; avoiding bad mistakes; and financing of a car to park in the garage. There are no links to other related Web pages, but you may not need them.

Standard Features:

- Listing of mortgage sources
- Software calculation of mortgage rates and payments
- Interest rate trends
- Home value estimates
- Obtaining your own credit report
- Bookstore
- Home estimates
- Finding contractors
- Surveys of consumers on housing issues

www.mortgage-net.com

RPS RELOCATION RESOURCE

The RPS Relocation Resource is a Texas based company specializing in relocation consulting. The Web site is a window to their personalized, no charge, service. Their business model places RPS staff as coordinating intermediaries for individuals or companies needing relocation services. They maintain a network of service providers who meet their performance standards and compensate RPS for their work. The menus indicate that RPS can help with everything from financing a new mortgage to transporting the cat. From the number and quality of their clients, it could be worthwhile to explore outsourcing some of the relocation effort to full time professionals with a reputation to protect, both from a cost savings and employee good will point of view.

Standard Features:

- Relocation planning software
- Salary differences calculator
- Moving checklists
- New home search
- Bookstore
- School profiles
- Change of address service
- Relocation process articles
- Relocation forums

www.rpsrelocation.com

THE SCHOOL REPORT

One of the biggest challenges faced by adults with school aged children is to locate in a good school district. Many cross state or city relocations have been squashed due to the fear that parents have of the schools in the new town. The school report just might be a resource you can use. Enter a state and city and you are able to gather free reports on over 200 pieces of data from any school in America. Learn about average class size, population statistics, student/teacher ratio, even SAT scores.

Standard Features:

- Has maps of each school district along with school address, principal, and phone number
- Reports are prepared that compare up to 6 schools and are mailed to users
- Links to home, mortgage, community, and child care resources for the school district in question are provided

www.nsrs.com

UHAUL MOVING ONLINE

The Uhaul Moving Online site promises to answer all the questions and provide most of the services associated with a relocation. The site is geared toward having the individual making the move taking the responsibility for handling the details of working with Uhaul. If moving the furniture is the major task of a relocation, using Uhaul can be a significant savings and the person making the change will have more personal control of the adventure. The site is designed to make the paperwork end of the process as simple as possible.

Features are:

- Maps to indicate location of pickup sites for truck and other equipment, and for the drop off point as well
- Guidelines for determining size of the truck or trailers
- Clear statement of costs

www.uhaul.com

YAHOO! REAL ESTATE—CITY COMPARISON

So HR professional, you are trying to land that candidate from Alabama and get them to consider a move to the beautiful metropolis of Charlotte, North Carolina. You try to finalize the deal but lingering questions pop up: What about the high cost of living in Charlotte? Does not Charlotte have a higher rate of crime? What is the exact population of Charlotte? Yahoo! Real Estate City Comparison is the answer! Get up to date information on how dozens of American cities compare with a few keystrokes and clicks of a mouse.

Comparisons:

- Cooling Index
- Electricity Costs
- Heating Index
- Home Purchase Costs
- Median Family Inc.
- High School Grad. Rate
- Bachelor Degree Rate
- Job Growth
- Crime Index
- Auto Insurance Rates
- Average Commute Time

- Population Density
- Property Tax Rate
- Population
- Property Tax
- Local Income Tax
- State Income Tax
- Sunny days per year
- Annual Precipitation
- Air Quality
- Unemployment Rate

verticals.yahoo.com/cities

9

SALARY ADMINISTRATION INTERNET SITES

Few HR functions are performed so frequently and ineptly as salary administration. Indeed, this is one area that needs greater attention to detail. The salary administration sites outlined in this chapter are very thorough in their collective perspective.

The human resource professionals who do perform effectively in this pivotal but largely unrecognized role of salary administration will provide their companies with a dynamic advantage in today's marketplace. Wily veterans have already discovered that having a fair and competitive salary structure is much less expensive than bidding wars, 'feel good' morale builder programs, unfocused in house training, and desperate counter offers. Few strategies are more effective for retention of excellent personnel or more suitable for keeping the focus of knowledge workers on the work at hand. The sites in this chapter provide tools, insights, and links to other resources.

AMERICAN COMPENSATION ASSOCIATION

The American Compensation Association site is principally for its members, but some useful data can be obtained there if you have the right software – like the newest Netscape with Java capabilities and Adobe Acrobat. In some respects, the site serves to promote JavaScript software more than it does the ACA. Some of the more readily available resources are a compensation-related glossary of over 1,000 definitions, complete with cross-references to ACA publications and a job search site. Beyond those two very useful tools, the site should appeal most strongly to senior HR management staff and full time compensation specialists who are members of the ACA.

Standard Features:

- Bookstore
- Seminar listings and advertisements
- Certification descriptions (ACA)
- Advertising opportunities
- Membership information
- ACA events
- Glossary of compensation terminology
- Job site for compensation specialists

www.acaonline.org

NATIONAL COMPENSATION SURVEY

Whatever your compensation strategy is, its continuing execution will benefit from professional familiarity with comprehensive data on current status and significant trends. This Bureau of Labor Standards site has the information you need, and if the volume seems overwhelming at first, common sense dictates that we realize that only the largest conglomerates will need over 20% of the data found there. It is not that there is useless information there, but that the data that is priceless for one company can be completely irrelevant for many others.

Standard Features:

- Detailed compensation data by Metropolitan Statistical Area (MSA)
- Special notices
- Publications and other documents
- Related BLS programs

www.bls.gov/comhome.htm

SALARY AND BENEFITS SURVEY REPORTS

Abbott, Langer & Associates, Inc. produces this collection of reports. Designed for human resource professionals and covering approximately 300 benchmark jobs, the reports target the dominant positions in the current labor market and represent data collected from over 7,000 organizations. The complete reports can be ordered from this compensation related consulting firm, but the free report samples can be useful in themselves. The language and concepts used are familiar tools to human resource professionals working in compensation/salary administration. The organization of material makes quick searches practical and the Web site is mirrored to ensure prompt access of users. The sponsors establish a good balance between providing useful data as a professional courtesy and marketing their services.

Standard Features:

- Links to free sample reports and an ordering process for complete data
- Free catalogs
- Feedback capability
- Search engine for site
- Free email newsletter subscription

www.abbott-langer.com

WAGE WEB

Wage Web is a simple site with much utility to HR professionals. Wage Web lists national compensation data for 160 benchmark positions for free on the site. To gain access to more detailed salary survey information your organization will have to pay a $100 fee to become a member of the site. Members may view not only the National Data, but may also view by geography, size of organization or industry. As we go to press, Wage Web has signed up over 1,300 member organizations. Wage Web is a good place to go for organizations on a tight budget.

Standard Features:

- Minimum, mean, and maximum salary information for 160 benchmarked positions
- Job families include HR, Administrative, Finance, Information Management, Healthcare, Engineering, Sales/ Marketing, Manufacturing
- Job descriptions listed for all positions
- Inexpensive membership fee

www.wageweb.com

10

TRAINING/CAREER DEVELOPMENT INTERNET SITES

Within the scope of the sites in this chapter, the human resource professional can find almost everything needed to plan, manage, execute, and evaluate a comprehensive training program—except for the technical details of how to perform a specific job. In today's tight labor market and with existing educational systems having difficulty keeping pace with the technological changes that are constantly destroying old job responsibilities and creating brand new ones, many human resource functions will be faced with developing the staff readily available. The imposing challenge of training cost effectively, and soon enough to keep up with the demand, is a special challenge.

Doing some serious research on the Internet is a positive alternative to outsourcing most of your training, and if the only solid revelation you collect is the ongoing value of the training investment, you will not have wasted your time. The sites in this chapter provide a wealth of other insights as well and a lot of straightforward techniques.

AMERICAN SOCIETY FOR TRAINING AND DEVELOPMENT

The ASTD site combines some of the best and some of the not-so-great aspects of the training profession. For HR Web surfers with an interest or urgent need, they will find a modest amount of immediately useful data, an extensive bookstore, and a very useful guide for using the site. A plethora of cookies and an occasional misspelled word are a modest deterrent, but this is still a great starting place for HR professionals involved in training.

Standard Features:

- Bookstore
- Membership sign up
- Online job bank
- Seminar listings
- Comprehensive open discussion forum
- Coordinated programs with CCL, SHRM, and AQP
- Extensive Buyers' Guide for products and services
- Opportunities to participate in serious training studies

www.astd.org

ASK ERIC

Ask Eric is an effective portal to the world of education. With the growth of intellectual competence content in typical workplace jobs and an apparent decline in the quality of output from public educational systems, this site is a first stop for human

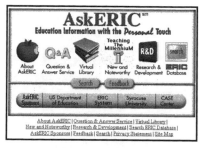

resource professionals making decisions about corporate education efforts. Despite an obvious emphasis on the education of children, this site can provide useful ideas and insights on training processes and objectives if some discretion is exercised on the age differences in learning modes. Ask Eric provides the links that make a difference. Corporate recruiters, for example, should check the site to determine which colleges have an effective IT skill development process. In addition to the text resources, the site describes the benefits to active participation in the education organization itself. Human resources professionals tasked with outreach projects to the local public education process will find the site to have significant resources.

Standard Features:

- A huge database of educational resources
- A search engine for quick access to materials
- U.S. Department of Education support
- Listserve on education issues

www.askeric.org

GRADSCHOOLS.COM

By our very nature, HR professionals are often involved in training and educational pursuits for employees within our organizations. A very handy reference tool to have at your side is gradschools.com. In this site you will find information on over 48,000 graduate programs worldwide. One key feature we especially like is the directory of "distance learning" programs. With a few clicks of a mouse you will be able to search not only traditional graduate programs, but programs geared to the busy working professionals.

Standard Features:

- Information on thousands of graduate programs
- Search site by type of program
- View programs geared to working professionals
- Graduate school discussion list available
- Links to other related sites
- Information on financial aid provided

www.gradschools.com

PETERSONS.COM—THE EDUCATION SUPERSTORE

As the site title indicates, Petersons is a portal site with links to a complete spectrum of educational opportunities, from graduate schools to summer camps. The online and distance learning resources are of particular interest to HR professionals because of the frequent need to upgrade the skills of current staff. The database of available institutions and their curriculums, cross  linked to valuable skills and individual assessments of the candidates can abbreviate the search process significantly. Excellent and lengthy articles supplement the research process with concepts and current news. A key word search engine expedites the selection as well. The site also covers undergraduate, graduate, executive, overseas study, and summer camps. A linked job site even allows graduates to put their new skills on the market if they must.

Standard Features:

- Multiple learning institutions and related resources
- Assessment and admission test tools
- Search engines
- Job site

www.petersons.com

SEMINAR INFORMATION SERVICE

The Seminar Information Service Web site is an abridged Internet version of an old standby for corporate seminar researchers, the SIS Workbook. There is a CD-ROM copy that includes all 200,000 of the current list, but you can get a lot of the same benefits on the Web site. By entering category, subcategory, city, state, date, or any combination in the search engine, you can find most of the topics that would appeal to HR professionals. For example, a quick search under human resource management resulted in 1,775 titles for calendar year 2000. Needless to say, there is a seminar somewhere on non-HR topics that would be worthwhile for other personnel at your company. The search engine is intuitive and you can search by sponsor or topic. A pull down menu or a key word search can be utilized. The site is an elegantly uncomplicated tool for seminar research.

Standard Features:

- Excellent search engine
- Extensive choices
- Online seminar sign up
- Online ordering of both CD-ROM and hard copy version of the SIS Workbook

www.seminarinformation.com

TEST.COM

Test.com is a Web site that provides a broad spectrum of practice tests for academic, professional, college entrance, programming, educator qualification, and others. As a portal and information site on testing in general, it seems to have no peer on the Internet. Thousands of secure, interactive, instantly scored tests and practice tests are available at a cost that is far less than practice exam books and complicated

software. And they are valid and reliable. They come from test publisher and writer partners. Their focus is on:

- HR managers and search firms
- job seekers and employees
- trade associations, government agencies and other institutions
- schools and students
- professionals who need to pass a licensing or certification test

Companies and schools can establish private accounts and customized test centers to structure testing programs specific to their needs.

Standard Features:

- Hundreds of online assessments available
- Organizations can build own test center

THE TRAINERS WAREHOUSE

The Trainers Warehouse Web site is a discount store for all the tools that professional presenters can use in their work. Customers can range from public school teachers to sales speakers and business strategy consultants. The site allows the ordering of software, hardware, hard copy materials, and books on presentation techniques. Costs range from $8.95 for a mouse pad to over $1000 for CBT software. You can order pointers, black boards, white boards, overhead projectors, and almost anything else instructional that one can imagine for the classroom or board room. It is a good place to check for products and prices before you patronize a local vendor.

Standard Features:

- Online catalog
- Online ordering
- Competitive pricing

www.trainerswarehouse.com

THE TRAINING REGISTRY

The Training Registry Web site is a serious and comprehensive supermarket for training products and services from online courses to training administration. Unlike the Training Warehouse that focused on resources for trainers, this site is a reservoir of outsourced training services as well as more tangible products. This is one of several highly competitive training resource sites that HR pros should check before making large cost commitments to vendors.

Standard Features:

- Directories and lists of courses, providers, products, and facilities
- Directories of speakers, consultants, and training associations
- A bookstore with more books on training than you will ever read
- A short listing of jobs available for qualified trainers

TRAINING & DEVELOPMENT COMMUNITY CENTER

The Training & Development Community Center is a portal for all kinds of books, publications, ideas, articles, recruiting, jobs, and usenet news groups— and all of them relate to training. In addition to selling a lot of good stuff, the site provides definitions of training terms, insights into the professional challenges, The site also performs the valuable function of highlighting the professional services of outstanding training providers. There are also useful links to multiple resources outside the site.

Standard Features:

- A job site is included
- Links to T & D professionals
- Bookstore
- T & D business supplier links
- Chat page, discussion groups, and usenet news groups
- Conferences
- Administrative Assistant software
- Excellent articles on the training profession

www.tcm.com/trdev

TRAINING NET

The Training Net is another all purpose training resource site. They claim to be the number one online marketplace for skills training and professional education—with the most comprehensive selection of all brands and forms of training, including classroom, on-site, and on-line training, books, videos, and CD-ROMs. They offer hundreds of thousands of course events annually in over 25 categories, and 1,000-plus of the market's leading training providers. TrainingNet offers an effective way to link the 54 million-plus professionals seeking training to the most comprehensive e-commerce marketplace for skills training and professional education.

Standard Features:

- Classroom courses
- Online events
- Computer based training
- Books
- CD ROMS, videos, and audio tapes

www.trainingnet.com

TRAINING SUPERSITE

The Training Supersite is an electic and comprehensive selection of training resources. The number of good training resource sites makes it imperative that HR pros experiment periodically to determine which is most effective for their organization. This one has all of the typical resources plus a few special ones.

Standard Features:

- A training mall with a big store and software download capacity
- A learning center with conference and other events listed
- A publications center
- A job site for connecting employers and trainers
- A community center with association directory and training sites
- Training sites rated
- Miscellaneous help software products

www.trainingsupersite.com

ABOUT THE AUTHORS

RAY SCHREYER

Ray Schreyer has over 20 years of experience in Human Resources, Staffing, Change Management, and most recently, Internet Recruiting Strategies. Significant employers have included such firms as IBM, Union Carbide, Union Oil Company, BASF, and First Union National Bank. He was one of the first individuals in America to recognize the significant impact of Internet Recruiting and served as a content provider to America Online's Career Center and as the Director of New Business for Monster.com in the mid 90's.

Ray received his masters training in Industrial/Organizational Psychology from the University of North Carolina. He is co-author of *The Employer's Guide to Recruiting On the Internet* and *Recruit and Retain the Best*. A native of Chicago, he migrated to the Carolinas in the mid 80's and fell in love with the hospitality and lifestyle of the community. He currently resides in Matthews, North Carolina with his wife Gayle. Ray can be reached via email at: nccareer@aol.com.

JOHN LEWIS MCCARTER JR.

John McCarter is a management consultant with broad experience in both human resources and industrial engineering. As a consultant with H. B. Maynard & Company, he worked with a broad variety of industrial concerns in productivity and labor incentive development, performing wage surveys and job evaluations for various clients. He also served as Senior Instructor at the Maynard Management Institute and taught hundreds of engineers and other management professionals work measurement technology. Clients included Wean United, Oklahoma Gas & Electric, Smith and Wesson, and Masland Carpet. He is a qualified instructor in all the Maynard Operations Sequence Techniques (MOST) systems.

At Charles Brooks Associates, John developed extensive operations training programs for the banking and automotive industries, and worked with Service Dimensions Inc. as well. Leading banking clients include Chemical Bank, NationsBank (now Bank of America), First American, and Manufacturers Hanover Bank. Industrial clients are General Motors and Siemens Automotive.

John McCarter is a team oriented professional, providing active leadership of client teams to accomplish challenging goals on time while developing the technical and management capacities of team members. He is an innovator in the creating of incentive programs for traditionally non-incentive jobs and an insightful organizer of job duties and responsibilities. John is also an outplacement specialist and a co-author of *The Employers' Guide to Recruiting on the Internet* and *Recruit and Retain the Best*.

He is a native of the Carolinas, a graduate of Clemson University, and the Belk College of Business, University of North Carolina at Charlotte. A long time resident of Charlotte, he is an avid reader and student of politics. He can be reached via email at: career@bellsouth.net.

Appendix
700+ Recruiting Sites

With the economy growing in size and complexity much faster than the supply of talented and eager human resources, we are supplementing the Top 100 Internet Web Site resources with over seven hundred additional recruiting sites. These are the sites where you can place your job ads and/or search for resumes. Sites are categorized according to site focus. Examples are "general" sites which are the supermarkets of job boards containing hundreds of types of jobs from all locations, to specific "regional" or "niche" based sites that serve a particular occupation or region of the country or world.

This list is by no means complete. Hundreds of other sites are in existence for every conceivable occupation and region of the world. We hope this list serves as a starting point. For help in utilizing those sites that meet your special needs, we recommend two other books—*The Employers' Guide to Recruiting on the Internet* and *Recruit and Retain the Best*. Yes, we wrote them as well, and hope that the coherent concepts and practical tactics will be of great value to you.

Accounting

Accounting Net .... www.accountingnet.com
Accounting.com .... www.accounting.com
American Assoc. of Financial Accounting .... www.aafa.com
RAW—The Accounting Web .... www.rutgers.edu/Accounting/raw

Advertising

Ad Week .... www.adweek.com
Advertising Age Job Bank .... adage.com/job_bank

Agriculture

Ag Related Jobs .... www.atinet.org/jobs
Am. Ag. Economics Assn. .... www.aaea.org/employment.html
College of Food, Agricultural,
   and Environmental Sciences .... cfaes.ohio-state.edu/career
eHarvest .... careers.eharvest.com
Positions in Weed Science (WeedJobs) .... www.nrcan.gc.ca/~bcampbel

Architecture

AIA Online .... www.aiaonline.com
American Planning Association .... www.planning.org/switchbd/jobs.html
American Society of Landscape Architects .... www.asla.org
E-Architect .... www.e-architect.com
"Job Hunting for Planning,
   Architects, etc." .... www.lib.berkeley.edu/ENVI/jobs.html
Architecture
AEC Job Bank .... www.aecjobbank.com

Arts

BackStage Online .... www.backstage.com
Casting Net .... www.castingnet.com
Creative Freelancers Online .... www.freelancers.com
Hollywood Web .... www.hollywoodweb.com
Playbill.. www.playbill.com
ShowBizJobs.com .... www.showbizjobs.com
Talent Works: The Online Casting Source .... www.talentworks.com

Aviation

Aero Jobs .... www.aerojobs.com
Aero World Net... www.aeroworldnet.com/jobops.htm
Airline Employment Assistance Corps .... www.avjobs.com
Airparts.com
Employment Guide .... www.airparts.com/employ/employ_index.cgi
Am. Instit. of Aeronautics & Astronautics .... www.aiaa.org
Aviation Communication .... www.flightinfo.com

Aviation Employee Placement Service .... www.aeps.com/aeps/aepshm.html
Corporate Aviation Resume Exchange .... www.scendtek.com/care
Space Careers .... www.spacelinks.com/SpaceCareers
Space Jobs .... www.spacejobs.com
The Mechanic .... www.the-mechanic.com

Clerical

Admin Exchange .... www.adminexchange.com
Au Pair in Europe .... www.princeent.com/aupair

Construction

American Public Works Association .... www.pubworks.org
Civil Projects .... www.civilprojects.com
Construction Job Store .... www.constructionjobstore.com
Engineering News-Record .... www.enr.com
Hard Hats Online .... www.hardhatsonline.com
Public Works Online .... www.publicworks.com/content/homepage
Right of Way .... www.rightofway.com

Convention Management

Convention Management Association .... www.pcma.org

Cruise Line

Cruise Line Jobs .... www.cruiselinejobs.com

Economic Development

American Economic Development Council .... www.aedc.org

Economists

E-JOE [European version] .... www.inomics.com/query/show?what=ejoe

JOE—Job Openings for Economists .... www.eco.utexas.edu/joe

Education

Academic Employment Network .... www.academploy.com
Academic Position Network .... www.apnjobs.com
AECT Placement Center ..... www.aect.org/Employment/Employment.htm
ASEE Career Scope .... www.asee.org/publications/html/classifieds.htm
CASE Jobs Classified .... www.case.org
Chronicle of Higher Education .... chronicle.com/jobs
Education JobSite .... www.edjobsite.com
Higher Ed Jobs .... www.higheredjobs.com
International Academic Job Market ... www.camrev.com.au/share/jobs.html
Jobs for the Association for
    Institutional Research .... www.airweb.org/jobs.html

Jobs In Higher Education .... www.gslis.utexas.edu/~acadres/jobs
K12Jobs www.k12jobs.com/
National Association of Personnel Admin. .... www.naspa.org
National Council of Teachers of Math .... www.nctm.org/jobs
National Educators Employment Review .... www.teacherjobs.com
Natl. Assoc. of College Business Officers .... www.nacubo.org
Oregon School Personnel Assn. www.ospa.k12.or.us
Positions in Christian
   Higher Education .... www.gospelcom.net/cccu/fac-admi/jobpost.html
Private School Employment Network .... www.privateschooljobs.com
State University Positions
   in Florida .... www.borfl.org/EmploymentOps/empframe.htm
Women In Higher Education .... www.wihe.com/index.htm
O-Hayoui Sensei English Teachers in Japan .... www.ohayosensei.com

Electricians
National Electrical Contractors Association .... www.necanet.org

Energy
Drilling Research Institute .... www.drillers.com/classifi.htm
eMine.com .... www.emine.com
Energyjobs.com .... www.energyjobs.com
InfoMine .... www.infomine.com
Mining USA .... www.miningusa.com/default.asp
Offshore Guides .... OffshoreGuides.com
Oil Link .... www.oillink.com
Petroleum Place .... www.discoveryplace.com

Engineering
Association of Facilities Engineers .... www.afe.org
Am. Soc. of Mechanical Engineers .... www.asme.org/jobs
Association for Higher Education Facilities Officers .... www.appa.org/
daVinci Times .... www.daVinciTimes.org
EE Times .... www.eet.com
Electronic News .... electronicnews.com
Engineering Job Source .... www.engineerjobs.com
EngineeringJobs.com .... www.engineeringjobs.com
Graduating Engineer .... www.careertech.com
IEEE USA Employment .... www.ieeeusa.org
Institute of Electronic & Electrical Engineers .... www.ieee.org
Materials Science and Engineering Jobs doL1.eng.sunysb.edu/jobs-grad.html
National Society of Black Engineers .... www.nsbe.org
National Society of Professional Engineers .... www.nspe.org
Society of Women Engineers .... www.swe.org

Facilities

Assn. Of Higher Education Facilities Officers .... www.appa.org
FacilitiesNet .... www.facilitiesnet.com/fn
FM Link .... www.fmlink.com
International Facilities management Assn. .... www.ifma.org

Fashion

Fashion Exchange .... www.fashionexch.com
Womens Wear Daily Classifieds .... wwd.com/classified/class.htm

Financial

100 Careers on Wall Streetwww.global+C5villager.com/villager/WSC.html
American Banker Career Zone .... www.americanbanker.com
Bloomberg Online .... www.bloomberg.com/fun/jobs.html
CFO Magazine .... www.cfonet.com/html/cfojobs.html
Financial Job Network .... www.financialjobnet.com
FinancialJobs.com .... www.financialjobs.com
FinCareer.com .... www.fincareer.com
Jobs for Bankers .... www.bankjobs.com
Mortgage Job Store .... www.mortgagejobstore.com
National Banking Network .... nbn-jobs.com
Tax-Jobs.Com .... www.tax-jobs.com
Treasury Management Association .... www.afponline.org

Food Service

American Culinary Federation .... www.acfchefs.org
Bakery Net .... www.bakery-net.com
Professional Brewers Page .... probrewer.com
Star Chefs .... www.starchefs.com
Supermarket News .... www.supermarketnews.com

Franchise

Be the Boss .... www.betheboss.com

Funeral

Funeral Net .... www.funeralnet.com

General

4Work www.4work.com
6figure Jobs www.6figurejobs.com
Alumnae Resources .... www.ar.org
AmericanJobs.com .... www.americanjobs.com
America's Job Bank .... www.ajb.dni.us
America's Online Help Wanted www2.ohw.com
Americas's Employers .... www.americasemployers.com

Best Jobs USA .... www.bestjobsusa.com
Boldface Jobs .... www.boldfacejobs.com
BridgePath Employment Services .... www.bridgepath.com
BusinessWeek Online Career Center .... www.businessweek.com/careers
Career Avenue .... www.careeravenue.com
Career Buzz .... www.careerbuzz.com
Career City .... www.careercity.com
Career Exposure .... www.careerexposure.com
Career Index .... www.careerindex.com
Career Link USA .... www.careerlinkusa.com
Career Search .... www.careersearch.net
Career Shop .... www.careershop.com
CareerBuilder .... www.careerbuilder.com
CareerCast .... www.careercast.com
CareerFile .... www.careerfile.com
CareerGuide .... www.careerguide.com
CareerMagazine .... www.careermag.com
CareerMart .... www.careermart.com
CareerMosaic .... www.careermosaic.com
CareerPath .... www.careerpath.com
CareerSite .... www.careersite.com
CareerWeb .... www.cweb.com
Classified Warehouse .... search.classifiedwarehouse.com
Classifieds2000 .... www.classifieds2000.com
direct-jobs.com .... www.direct-jobs.com
Drake Beam Morin .... www.dbm.com/dbm.html
Electronic News OnLine .... www.electronicnews.com
Employment Weekly .... www.employment-weekly.com
Entry Level Jobs www.urban.org/employment/brochure1/index.htm
Excite Classifieds www.classifieds2000.com
Future Access Employment Guide . www.futureaccess.com:80/employ.html
GetMeAJob .... www.getmeajob.com
Go Jobs: The Guide to Online Jobs .... www.gojobs.com
Good Works .... www.essential.org/goodworks
HeadHunter.NET .... www.headhunter.net
Heart .... www.career.com
Help Wanted .... www.helpwanted.com
Help-Wanted USA .... www.iccweb.com
Hot Jobs .... www.hotjobs.com
Job Bank USA .... www.jobbankusa.com
Job Exchange .... www.jobexchange.com
Job Hunt .... www.job-hunt.org
JobOptions .... www.joboptions.com
Jobs.com .... www.jobs.com
Monster.com .... www.monster.com
National Business Employment Weekly .... www.nbew.com
NationJob Network .... www.nationjob.com

Net Temps .... www.net-temps.com
Passport Access .... www.passportaccess.com
Recruiters Online Network .... www.ipa.com
ResumeLink .... resume-link.com
Shawn's Internet Executive Resume Center .... www.inpursuit.com/sirc
SmartPost Network .... www.smartpost.com
Talent Hunter www.3dsite.com/ism/resumes/cgi-bin/talent-hunter
Telecomuting Jobs .... www.tjobs.com/jobopps.htm
The Career Connection .... www.connectme.com
Yahoo! Careers .... careers.yahoo.com

General—CEO

CEO Job Opportunity Update .... www.associationjobs.com

General—College Grads

Branch Out .... www.branchout.com
College Central Network .... www.collegecentral.com
College Connection www.careermosaic.com/cm/cc/cc1.html
College Grad Job Hunter .... www.collegegrad.com
College Net .... www.collegenet.com
College News Online .... www.collegenews.com/jobs.htm
JobDirect.com .... www.jobdirect.com
JobTrak .... www.jobtrak.com
JobWeb .... www.jobweb.org
National Alumni Placement Association .... www.careers.com
The Job Resource .... www.thejobresource.com

General—Diversity

Bilingual-Jobs .... www.bilingual-jobs.com
Black Collegian .... www.black-collegian.com
Black E.O.E. Journal .... www.blackeoejournal.com/jobsearch.html
Black Voices .... www.blackvoices.com
Career Center for Workforce Diversity .... www.eop.com
Career Women .... www.careerwomen.com
Careers Online www.disserv3.stu.umn.edu/COL
Diversilink .... www.diversilink.com
Diversity Careers Online .... www.diversitycareers.com
Diversity Employment .... www.diversityemployment.com
Diversity Link .... www.diversitylink.com/index.htm
Feminist Career Center www.feminist.org/911/911jobs.html
GayWork.com .... www.gaywork.com
Hispanic Online .... www.hisp.com
LatinoWeb .... www.latinoweb.com/jobs/jobs.htm
LatPro .... www.latpro.com
Minorities Job Bank .... www.minorities-jb.com
National Black MBA Association .... www.nbmbaa.org

Saludos Web .... www.saludos.com
The Black Collegian Online .... www.blackcollegian.com
Women Connect.com .... www.womenconnect.com

General—Executive

Exec-U-Net.. www.execunet.com
Netshare .... www.netshare.com

General—Federal

Federal Jobs Digest .... www.jobsfed.com
Fedworld .... www.fedworld.gov/jobs/jobsearch.html
Jobs in Government .... www.jobsingovernment.com
USA Jobs from OPB .... www.usajobs.opm.gov

General—IT/Engineering

Contract Employment Weekly .... www.ceweekly.com

General—IT/MBA

CareerCentral .... www.careercentral.com

General—Non-Profit

Community Career Center .... www.nonprofitjobs.org
Opportunity Nocs .... www.opportunitynocs.org/home.html

General—Professional

Professional Career Network .... www.jobs-careers.com
Top Jobs USA .... www.topjobsusa.com
Wall Street Journal Interactive Edition .... careers.wsj.com

General—Resumes

America's Talent Bank .... www.atb.org

General—Summer Employment

Great Summer Jobs .... www.gsj.petersons.com
Summer Jobs .... www.summerjobs.com

Graphics

3D Site www.3dsite.com
Design Sphere Online .... www.dsphere.net/comm/jobs.html
MipMap Recruiting .... www.mipmap.com

Hospitality

Casino Careers .... www.casinocareers.com
Hospitality Net .... www.hospitalitynet.org

Hotel Online .... www.hotel-online.com/Neo
Resortjobs.com .... www.resortjobs.com

Human Resources

American Compensation Association .... www.acaonline.org
American Society for Training
  and Development .... www.astd.org/virtual_community
BenefitsLink .... www.benefitslink.com
Employee Benefit News .... www.benefitnews.com/index.cfm
HR COMM .... www.hrcomm.com
HR Network .... www.hrreport.com
HR Recruiting .... hr-recruiting.com
HR World... www.hrworld.com
HRIM Mall... www.hrimmall.com
HRSites... www.hrsites
Instructional Systems
  Technology .... education.indiana.edu/ist/students/jobs/joblink.html
International Personnel Management Association .... www.ipma-hr.org
Job Postings for Benefits
  and Human Resources .... www.ifebp.org/jobs/index.html
Jobs 4 HR www.jobs4hr.com
Northeast Human Resource Association .... www.nehra.com
SHRM HR Jobs .... www.shrm.org
TCM's HR Careers .... www.tcm.com/hr-careers
Training Net .... www.trainingnet.com
Training Supersite Job Bank .... www.trainingsupersite.com/jobs

Industrial

Finishing.com .... www.finishing.com
Food and Drug Packaging .... www.fdp.com
HVACJob.. www.hvacjob.com

Industrial Design

Core Industrial Design www.core77.com

Industrial Equipment

trans-ACTION .... www.trans-action.com

Information Technology

100 Careers In Cyperspace .... www.globalvillager.com/villager/CSC.html
AIA Computer Jobs .... www.aiacomputerpros.net
Association for Computing
  Machinery (ACM).. www.acm.org/cacm/careeropps
Association for Women in Computing .... www.awc-hq.org
Association of Online Professionals .... www.aop.org

AutoCAD Job Network .... www.acjn.com
BizTech Network .... www.brint.com
Black Data Processing Association Online .... www.bdpa.org
Career NET .... www.careernet.com
CareerExchange .... www.careerexchange.com
CATIA Job Network CAD/CAM/CAE .... www.catjn.com
Chicago Software Newspaper CareerCat .... www.chisoft.com
Computer Work .... www.computerwork.com
Computer World's IT Careers .... www.computerworld.com
Computing Research Association
    job listings .... www.cra.org/main/cra.jobs.html
Developers.net .... www.developers.net
DICE High Tech Jobs Online .... www.dice.com
Dr. Dobb's Journal .... www.ddj.com
Federal Computer Week .... www.fcw.com
Hi Tech Career Centre .... www.hitechcareer.com
Ideas Job Network CAD/CAM/CAE .... www.ideasjn.com
IEEE Computer Listing .... computer.org/careers
Industry Standard .... www.thestandard.com
Information Week .... www.informationweek.com/career
Infoworld .... www.infoworld.com
Internation Assn. For HR Information Mgmt. .... www.ihrim.com
Internet World .... jobs.internet.com
InternetWeek Career Search .... www.internetwk.com/bestjobs/career.htm
ITTA .... www.it-ta.com
Java World .... www.javaworld.com
Job Engine .... www.jobEngine.com
Jobs for Programmers www.jfpresources.com/jobtele1.html
Information TechnologyJobWarehouse .... www.jobwarehouse.com
Mactalent.com .... www.mactalent.com
Oracle Search .... www.orasearch.com
Pro/E Job Network CAD/CAM/CAE .... www.pejn.com
SelectJOBS .... www.selectjobs.com
Software Contractors' Guild .... www.scguild.com
SolidWorks Job Network CAD/CAM/CAE .... www.swjn.com
Surf-IT.com .... www.surfit.com
Techies.com .... www.techies.com
TechJobs SuperSite .... supersite.net/techjobs
The ComputerJobs Store .... www.computerjobs.com
The RS/6000 Employment Page www.s6000.com/job.html
The Software Quality
    Institute Job Links .... www.utexas.edu/coe/sqi/joblink/joblink.html
UG Job Network CAD/CAM/CAE .... www.ugjn.com
US Job Network High Tech Job & Resume Bank .... www.usjob.net
Web Jobs USA .... www.webjobsusa.com
Westech's Virtual Job Fair .... www.vjf.com
Windows for Jobs .... www.delphi.com/windowsforjobs

Windows NT Resource Center .... www.bhs.com/default.asp
Women In Technology & Industry .... www.witi.com

Insurance
Insurance Connections .... www.connectyou.com/ins

Interior Design
International Interior Design Assn. .... www.iida.org

Job Resources
Internet Job Source .... statejobs.com
Job Resources by
    US Region .... www.wm.edu/csrv/career/stualum/jregion.html
Jobs & Career Links .... www.owt.com/jobsinfo/jobsinfo.htm

Journalism
American Journalism Review Online .... www.newslink.org/joblink.html
E & P Classified .... epclassifieds.com/cgi-bin/nclassyEPM.x/epmXCT
JAWS Job Bank .... www.jaws.org/jobs.shtml
Journalism Job Bank .... www.journalism.berkeley.edu/jobs
National Diversity
    Newspaper Job Bank .... www.newsjobs.com/jobs/jobs.html
Society for Technical Communications .... www.stc-va.org/default.htm

Land Surveying
Land Surveyors .... www.landsurveyors.com

Legal
Cop Spot www.cop-spot.com/cop-spot/index2.html
Cops Online .... www.copsonline.com
Law Employment Center .... www.lawjobs.com
National Directory of Emergency Services www1.firejobs.com/ndes
National Federation of Paralegals .... www.paralegals.com
Officer.com .... www.officer.com
Security Jobs Network .... securityjobs.net
The Blue Line .... www.theblueline.com
The Federal Judiciary .... www.uscourts.gov
US Department of Justice www.usdoj.gov/06employment/index.html

Library
American Association of Law Libraries .... www.aallnet.org/index.asp
American Library Association .... www.ala.org/education
ARLIS/NA Job Net .... www.arlisna.org/jobs.html
Librarian Job Search Source .... www.lisjobs.com

Library Job Posting
on the Net .... topcat.bridgew.edu/~snesbeitt/libraryjobs.htm
Library of Congress .... lcweb.loc.gov/homepage/about.html#working

Library—Music

Music Library Association .... www.musiclibraryassoc.org/se_job.htm

Linguists

EFLWEB .... www.u-net.com/eflweb/home.htm
Jobs in Linguistics .... www.linguistlist.org/jobsindex.html
Jobs in Russia and
East Central Europe ..... www.departments.bucknell.edu/russian/jobs.html
The ESL Café's Job Center .... eslcafe.com/jobs

Machinist

Machinists' Exchange Online .... www.machinist.net/default.htm

Management

Am. Soc. Of Assn. Executives .... www.asaenet.org/careerheadquarters
Direct Marketing World Job Center .... www.dmworld.com
Equipment Leasing Association Online .... www.elaonline.com
International Assn. of Conference Centers . www.iacconline.com/home.cfm
International Society for Performance Improvement .... www.ispi.org
National Assn. Of Purchasing Mgmt. .... www.napm.org

Manufacturing

Job Search .... www.manufacturing.net/resources/jobs/default.htm

Marketing

MarketingJobs.com .... www.marketingjobs.com

MBA Grads

MBA Careers .... www.mbacareers.com
MBA Employment Connection Association .... www.mbanetwork.com
MBA free Agents.com .... www.mbafreeagents.com
MBA job.com .... www.mbajob.com

Media

Airways Media Web .... www.airwaves.com
AJR Newslink Job Link .... ajr.newslink.org/joblink.html
America's TV Job Network .... www.tvjobnet.com
Broadcast Employment Center .... www.tvjobs.com
Media Week .... www.mediaweek.com

Medical

Allied Health Opportunities .... www.gvpub.com
American College of Nurse Midwives .... www.midwife.org/prof
American Massage Theraphy Assn. .... www.amtamassage.org
American Medical Association .... www.ama-assn.org
American Physical Therapy Association .... www.apta.edoc.com
Career Expresso .... www.sph.emory.edu/studentservice/Career.html
Emergency Medicine Practice Opportunity www.embbs.com/job/jobs.html
Emergency Physician .... www.edphysician.com
Experimental Medical
  Job Listings .... www.medcor.mcgill.ca/EXPMED/DOCS/jobs.html
Fairview RehabQuest .... rehabquest.com/home.html
Health Care Job Store .... www.healthcarejobstore.com
Health Care Jobs Online .... www.hcjobsonline.com
Health Care Source .... www.healthcaresource.com
Health Careers Online .... www.healthcareers-online.com/Welcome.htm
HealthOpps .... www.healthopps.com
International Pharmaccutical .... www.pharmajobs.com/index.html
Med Connect .... www.medconnect.com
MedHunters .... www.medhunters.com
Medical Device Link .... www.dcvicelink.com/career
Medzilla .... www.medzilla.com
Monster Health Care .... healthcare.monster.com
New England Journal of Medicine .... www.nejm.org
Nurse Jobs .... www.nurse-jobs.com
Nursing Spectrum .... www.nursingspectrum.com
Nursing-Jobs.com .... www.nursing-jobs.com/index.html
Pharmacy Week .... www.pharmacyweek.com
Physicians Employment .... www.physemp.com
Rehab Options .... www.rehaboptions.com

Medical—Academia

Academic Physician & Scientist .... www.acphysci.com

Medical—Mental Health

Mental Health Net .... mentalhelp.net/joblink

Military

Navy .... www.navyjobs.com
The Defense Industry .... www.us.net/marylandcareers/intel.html
US Air force Employment Home Page .... www.af.mil/careers

Military Transition

Corporate Gray Online .... www.greentogray.com
Defense Outplacement Referral System .... www.dmdc.osd.mil/dors

Museum

Museum Employment Resource Center .... w3.trib.com/~jamesal

Music

American Symphony Orch. .... www.symphony.org
Musical Online .... www.musicalonline.com

NonProfits

ExecSearches .... www.execsearches.com/exec
Philanthrophy News Digests .... fdncenter.org/pnd/current/index.html

Oceanography

Am. Soc. of Limnology & Oceanography .... aslo.org/jobs.html
American Fisheries Society Jobs Bulletin .... www.fisheries.org/jobs.html
Zoo and Aquarium Job Listings .... www.aza.org/communique/positions

Packaging

PackInfo World .... www.packinfo-world.com/WPO

Plastics

PolySort .... www.polysort.com

Psychology

APA Monitor Classified Advertising .... www.apa.org/ads
PsycCareers .... www.psyccareers.com/Asecured/index.cfm

Purchasing

National Assn. of
   Purchasing Managers—New York .... www.napm-ny.org/CareerHub.htm
National Assn. of
   Purchasing Managers—Silicon Valley .... www.catalog.com/napmsv

Real Estate

Natl. Assn. Of Corp. Real Estate Executives .... www.nacore.com
Real Estate Job Store .... www.realestatejobstore.com
Real Jobs—Real Estate Jobs .... www.real-jobs.com

Regional—Africa

Africa Job and Career Center .... www.search-beat.com/africajobs.htm
Africa Online Jobs .... www.AfricaOnline.com

Regional—Alabama

Alabama Job Bank .... www.dir.state.al.us/es
Alabama State Employment Job Search .... al.jobsearch.org
AlaWeb [Alabama] .... www.state.al.us

Regional—Alaska

Alaska Jobs Center .... www.juneau.com/alaskajobs
Alaska's Job Bank .... labor-aix.state.ak.us/cgi-bin/jobs
Anchorage Daily News .... www.and.com
State of Alaska Jobs .... www.jobs.state.ak.us

Regional—Arizona

Arizona Careers Online .... www.diversecity.com/jobs.html
Arizona Daily Star .... www.azstarnet.com
Arizona State Job Bank .... az.jobsearch.org

Regional—Arkansas

Arkansas Employment Register .... www.arjobs.com
Arkansas Job Bank .... ar.jobsearch.org
Arkansas State Job Bank .... www.state.ar.us/esd

Regional—Asia

Asia Online—
    Asia Emploment Center .... asiadragons.com/employment/home.shtml
Asia-Net .... www.asia-net.com
Career China .... www.globalvillager.com/villager/CC.html

Regional—Australia

Careermosaic Australia .... www.careermosaic.com.au
Cowley Job Centre .... www.cowleys.com/au/public/jobs.htm
Employment in Australia .... www.employment.com.au
Monster Australia .... www.monster.com.au

Regional—Belgium

Monster Belgium .... www.monster.be

Regional—California

680 Careers www.680careers.com
BAJobs (SF Bay Area Jobs) .... www.bajobs.com
BayAreaCareers.com .... www.bayareacareers.com
Cal State University
    Employment Board Job Hunt .... www.csueb.sfsu.edu/jobs.html
California Jobs... www.Californiajobs.com
California Journalism Job Bank .... www.cxne.org/csne/postingfees.html
California State Government .... www.ca.gov
California State Job Bank .... ca.jobsearch.org
CLNET .... www.latino.sscnet.ucla.edu
Jobs Jobs Jobs .... www.jobsjobsjobs.com
JobSmart California .... www.jobsmart.org
Los Angles Times .... www.latimes.com

Mercury Center Web .... www.sjmercury.com
San Diego Jobs .... www.sandiegojobs.com
San Francisco Chronicle Gateway .... www.sfna.com/cgi-bin/main.pl
The SofTech Jobs Board .... www.northbay.com/softech/index.html
Youth@Work .... www.youthatwork.org

Regional—Canada

ActiJob .... www.actijob.com
Canada Job .... www.canadajob.com
Career Bridge .... www.careerbridge.com
Career Connect .... www.theglobeandmail.com/careerconnect
Career Information of British Columbia .... www.lmcia.bc.ca
Career Internetworking .... www.careerkey.com
Careermosaic Canada .... www.canada.careermosaic.com
Monster Canada .... www.monster.ca
Net Jobs Information Services .... www.netjobs.com

Regional—Carolinas

CarolinaJobs.com .... www.carolinajobs.com
Carolinas Career Web .... www.carolinascareerweb.com

Regional—China

Career China .... www.globalvillager.com/villager/cc.html
The Daily Job .... www.dailyjob.com
Wang & Li Asia Resources .... www.wang-li.com

Regional—Colorado

Colorado Job Bank .... co.jobsearch.org
Colorado Jobs Information .... www.state.co.us.jobinfo.html
Colorado Online Job Connection .... coloradojobs.com

Regional—Connecticut

Connecticut Job Bank .... www.ctdol.state.ct.us
Hartford Courant .... www.courant.com

Regional—DC

District of Columbia Job Bank .... dc.jobsearch.org

Regional—Deleware

Virtual Career Network .... www.vcnet.net/default.asp

Regional—Europe

EuroJobs .... eurojobs.com
taps.com .... www.taps.com

Regional—Florida

Florida Career Link .... www.floridacareerlink.com
Orlando Sentinel .... www.orlandosentinel.com
OrlandoJobs.com .... www.orlandojobs.com/index-main.cfm
Sun-Sentinel .... www.sun-sentinel.com/careerpath
www.Floridajobs.org .... www.floridajobs.org

Regional—France

Careermosaic France .... www.careermosaic.tm.fr
Monster France .... www.monster.fr

Regional—Georgia

Atlanta's Computer Job Store .... www.atlanta.computerjobs.com
Georgia Dept. of Labor .... www.dol.state.ga.us/job_ops.htm

Regional—Hawaii

Hawaii Job Bank .... hi.jobsearch.org

Regional—Hong Kong

Careermosaic Hong Kong .... www.careermosaic.hk
Hong Kong Standard .... www.hkstandard.com
Recruit Online .... www.recruitonline.com

Regional—Idaho

Idaho Works .... www.doe.state.id.us

Regional—Illinois

ChicagoJobs .... www.chicagojobs.org
Illinois Dept. of Employment Services .... www.ides.state.il.us
The Chicago Tribune .... www.chicago.tribune.com

Regional—India

Career India .... www.careerindia.com
Cyber India Online .... www.ciol.com
India-NAUKRI .... www.naukri.com
WinJobs .... www.winjobs.com/marketing

Regional—Indiana

Indiana Job Bank .... in.jobsearch.org

Regional—Indonesia

IndoScape .... www.indoscape.com/cfo

Regional—International

Career Mosaic
   International Gateway .... www.careermosaic.com/cm/gateway
Eastern & Central Europe Job Bank .... www.ecejobbank.com
Expat Forum .... www.expatforum.com
International Jobs .... www.internationaljobs.org
Monster International .... international.monster.com/index.asp
Overseas Jobs Web .... www.overseasjobs.com
Russian & East European
   Institute Employment .... www.indiana.edu/~reeiweb/indemp.html

Regional—Iowa

Dubuque Iowa .... www.dubuque-ia.com/jobs.cfm
Iowa Jobs .... www.state.ia.us/jobs

Regional—Ireland

Irish Jobs .... www.exp.ie

Regional—Israel

Israel Jobnet .... www.jobnet.co.il

Regional—Japan

AEA Japan.. www.aea.or.jp
Careermosaic Japan .... www.careermosaic.or.ip
Jobs in Japan .... www.jobsinjapan.com/job-listings.htm

Regional—Kansas

Kansas Careers .... www.personal.ksu.edu/~dangle
Kansas Jobs .... www.kansasjobs.org

Regional—Kentucky

Kentucky Job Bank .... ky.jobsearch.org

Regional—Korea

Careermosaic Korea .... www.careermosaickorea.com

Regional—Louisiana

Louisiana Works .... www.ldol.state.la.us

Regional—Maine

Maine's Job Bank .... me.jobsearch.org

Regional—Malaysia

Malaysia Online .... www.mol.com

Regional—Maryland

Maryland's Careernet .... www.careernet.state.md.us
Maryland's Job Bank .... md.jobsearch.org

Regional—Massachusetts

Boston Globe .... www.boston.com
Boston Herald JobFind .... www.jobfind.com
Boston Job Bank .... www.bostonjobs.com
Boston Search.com .... www.bostonsearch.com
Mass Job Bank .... ma.jobsearch.org
Town Online .... www.townonline.com/working

Regional—Michigan

Michigan Works .... michworks.org

Regional—Minnesota

Adguide Employment Web Site .... www.adguide.com
Minnesota Dept. of Economic Security .... www.des.state.mn.us

Regional—Mississippi

Mississippi Job Search .... ms.jobsearch.org

Regional—Missouri

Missouri Works .... www.works.state.mo.us

Regional—Montana

Montana Job Service .... jsd.dli.state.mt.us

Regional—Nebraska

Access Omaha www.accessomaha.com:80
Nebraska Careerlink .... www.careerlink.org
Nebraska Job Bank .... ne.jobsearch.org

Regional—Netherlands

Monster Netherlands .... www.monsterboard.nl

Regional—Nevada

Nevada State Job Bank .... www.state.nv.us/detr/detr.html

Regional—New Hampshire

New Hampshire Works .... www.nhworks.state.nh.us

Regional—New Jersey

Employment Channel .... www.employ.com
New Jersey Online .... www.nj.com/careers
New Media Association of NJ .... www.nmanj.com
NJ Job Bank .... nj.jobsearch.org
NJ Jobs .... www.njjobs.com
Workforce New Jersey .... www.wnjpin.state.nj.us

Regional—New Mexico

New Mexico's Job Bank .... www.ajb.dni.us/nm

Regional—New York

New York Dept. of Labor .... www.labor.state.ny.us
New York Times .... www.nytimes.com
Smart Dog .... www.smartdog.org
Syracuse Online .... www.syracuse.com
Western New York Jobs .... www.wnyjobs.com

Regional—New Zealand

Careermosaic New Zealand .... www.careermosaic.co.nz
Job Net New Zealand .... www.jobnetnz.co.nz
Monster New Zealand .... www.monster.co.nz
Statistical Jobs in New Zealand
   and Australia .... www.maths.uq.edu.au/~gks/jobs

Regional—North Carolina

CarolinaJobs.com .... www.carolinajobs.com
News & Observer .... www.news-observer.com
North Carolina Employment Security Commission ...... www.esc.state.nc.us
Triangle Jobs.com .... www.trianglejobs.com

Regional—North Dakota

Job Service of North Dakota .... www.state.nd.us/jsnd

Regional—Ohio

Career Board .... www.careerboard.com
Columbus Dispatch .... www.dispatch.com
Ohio Bureau of Employment Resources .... www.state.oh.us/obes

Regional—Oklahoma

Oklahoma's Job Net .... www.oesc.state.ok.us/jobnet/default.htm

Regional—Oregon

Oregon Employment Department .... www.emp.state.or.us
PDX Jobs (Portland) .... www.pdxjobs.com

Regional—Overseas

Job Pilot .... www.jobpilot.net/index.phtml

Regional—Pennsylvania

Find a Job in Pittsburgh .... www.pghguide.com/pghjobs/jobsites.html
JobNet .... www.jobnet.com
Pennsylvania Job Bank .... www.ajb.dni.us/pa
Philly Works .... www.phillyworks.com
Philly.com .... www.philly.com

Regional—Quebec

Careermosaic Quebec .... www.careermosaicquebec.com

Regional—Rhode Island

Rhode Island Dept. of Labor & Training .... www.det.state.ri.us

Regional—Scandanavia

Nordic Jobfinder .... www.jobfinder.se

Regional—Singapore

BizLINKS .... sunflower.singnet.com.sg/~g6615000
Career Opportunities in Singapore .... www.singapore-careers.com
Careermosaic ASEAN (Singapore) .... www.careermosaic.com.sg
Monster Singapore .... www.monster.com.sg

Regional—South Africa

Job Navigator .... www.jobs.co.za

Regional—South Carolina

South Carolina Employment Security Commission .... www.sces.org

Regional—South Dakota

South Dakota's Job Bank .... www.ajb.dni.us/sd

Regional—Switzerland

Swiss Web Jobs .... www.swisswebjobs.ch/exec/index/swj/de

Regional—Tennessee

Tennessee Dept. of Employment Security .... www.state.tn.us/empsec

Regional—Texas

Dallas Morning News .... www.dallasnews.com
DFW Job Hotlines .... www.utdallas.edu/student/career/hotlines.html

Houston Chronicle Interactive .... www.chron.com
Texas Workforce Commission .... www.twc.state.tx.us

Regional—United Kingdom

Careermosaic United Kingdom .... www.careermosaic-uk.co.uk
Job Serve: IT in UK .... www.jobserve.com
Jobs Unlimites .... www.jobsunlimited.co.uk
Monster United Kingdom .... www.monster.co.uk
People Bank www.peoplebank.com/pbank/owa/pbk06w00.main

Regional—Utah

Utah's Job Connection .... www.dws.state.ut.us

Regional—Various

City Search .... www.citysearch.com

Regional—Vermont

Vermont Dept. of Employment & Training .... www.det.state.vt.us

Regional—Virginia

Virginia Employment Commission .... www.vec.state.va.us

Regional—Washington

Washington State Job Bank .... www.ajb.dni.us/wa

Regional—Washington DC

Washington Post .... www.washingtonpost.com/wp-adv/jobs

Regional—West Virginia

West Virginia Job Bank .... www.ajb.dni.us/wv

Regional—Wisconsin

Job File www.netsource-1.com/jobfiles/index.htm
Milwaukee Journal Sentinel .... www.onwis.com
Wisconsin Employment
    Connection .... www.dwd.state.wi.us/dwe-wec/default.htm
Wisconsin Jobs Online .... www.wisjobs.com

Regional—Wyoming

Wyoming Job Network .... wyjobs.state.wy.us

Religion

Christian Jobs Online .... www.christianjobs.com
Ministry Link .... www.csbsju.edu/sot/MinistryLink/Default.htm
MinistryConnect .... www.ministryconnect.org

Relocation

Employee Relocation Council .... www.erc.org
RelocationRetail JobNet .... www.retailjobnet.com/cf/main.cfm

Retail

Retail Seek .... www.retailseek.com/index.html

Safety

Safestyle.com .... www.safestyle.com/index.html

Sales

Sales .... www.salesseek.com/index.html
Sales Job.com .... www.salesjob.com

Science

Academe This Week .... chronicle.com/jobs
Acquatic Network .... www.aquanet.com
Am. Assoc. of Cereal Chemists .... www.scisoc.org/aacc
Am. Astronomical
   Society Job Register .... www.aas.org/JobRegister/aasjobs.html
Am. Statistical Assoc. Job Bank . www.amstat.org/opportunities/index.html
American Academy of Forensic Sciences .... www.aafs.org
American Chemical Career Society .... www.acs.org/careers
American Chemical Society (ACS) Job Bank .... pubs.acs.org/plweb
American Institute of Physics:
   Employment and Industry .... www.aip.org/careersvc
American Mathematical Society
   job listings .... www.ams.org/eims
American Society of Agronomy .... www.agronomy.org/career/career.html
Bio Online .... www.bio.com
BIOCareer Employment Center .... www.biocareer.com
Bioinformatics .... www.bioplanet.com/chat/jobs/index.html
BioMedNet .... www.biomednet.com/jobs
BioNet Employment
   Opportunities www.bio.net:80/hypermail/EMPLOYMENT
BioSpace Career Center .... www.biospace.com/job_index.cfm
Cell classified .... jobs.cell.com
Cell Press Online .... www.cellpress.com
Chemistry & Industry .... chemistry.mond.org
ChemistryJobs.com .... www.chemistryjobs.com
Computational Fluid Dynamics Online .... www.cfd-online.com
Cyber Sierra Natural Resources
   Job Search .... www.cyber-sierra.com/nrjobs/index.html
EarthWorks .... ourworld.compuserve.com/homepages/eworks
Ecological Society of America .... esa.sdsc.edu/jobs.htm
EE-link Grants and Jobs ..... www.eelink.net/grants-generalinformation.html

Employment Links for
Biomedical Scientist .... www.his.com/~graeme/employ.html
Environmental Careers .... www.eco.org
Environmental Careers World .... environmental-jobs.com
Etomological Society of America .... www.entsoc.org/careers
Experimental Partical
Physics jobs .... www-hep.colorado.edu/~bbehrens/rumor.html
"Forensics Laboratories, US Fish and Wildlife Services" ..... www.lab.fws.gov
Frontiers in Bioscience:
Jobs in biology .... www.bioscience.org/urllists/jobs.htm
Genome Jobs .... www.genomejobs.com
GeoJobSource .... www.geojobsource.com
GeoPlace Marketplace .... www.geoplace.com/marketplace/classified.asp
GeoSci Jobs Mailing
List Archeves .... www.eskimo.com/~tcsmith/mail/gsj-arc.html
GeoWeb .... www.ggrweb.com/job.html
GIS Jobs Clearinghouse .... www.gjc.org
GISRS Jobs .... www.eskimo.com/~tcsmith/mail/gisj-arc.html
HUM-MOLGEN .... www.hum-molgen.de/positions/index.html
Institute for
Operations Research ... www.anderson.ucla.edu/informs/career/joblist.htm
Institute of Physics .... www.iop.org
Instrument Society of America .... www.isa.org/classads
Job Listings at Dendrome .... dendrome.ucdavis.edu/jobs/index.html
Job Opportunities in
Entomology .... www.colostate.edu/Depts/Entomology/jobs/jobs.html
Materials Jobs .... www.welding-engineer.com/materialsjobs.html
Mathematical Association of
America jobs .... www.maa.org/pubs/employ.html
Medzilla/FSG Online .... www.chemistry.com
MET Jobs Mailing
List Archives .... www.eskimo.com/~tcsmith/mail/mj-arc.html
Nature Classified .... www.nature.com/jobs/index.html
New Scientist Jobs .... www.newscientistjobs.com/frame_regset.html
Optics.org .... optics.org/employment
"PhD's Org. Science, Math, and Engineering" .... www.phds.org
Physics Job Openings
by thread .... XXX.lanl.gov/Announce/Jobs/date.html#end
Physics Jobs .... physicsweb.org/jobs
PhysLink .... www.physlink.com/jobs.cfm
Plasma Gate (Physics) .... plasma-gate.weizmann.ac.il/Jobs.html
Science Online .... www.scienceonline.org
Scientific Professional Network .... recruit.sciencemag.org
Scijobs.org .... scijobs.org
Society of Industrial and
Applied Mathematics .... www.siam.org/profops/profops.htm
Statistics Job Announcements .... www.stat.ufl.edu/vlib/jobs.html

The American Society for Mass Spectromics .... www.asms.org/employ.html
The British Medical Journal .... classified.bmj.com
The Fed. of Am. Biologists for
    Experimental Biology ns2.faseb.org/career/index.html
The Internet Pilot to Physics .... physicsweb.org/TIPTOP

Social Service

Social Work / Service Jobs 128.252.132.4/jobs
SocialService.Com .... www.socialservice.com

Social Work

Federal Job Source .... dcjobsource.com/fed.html
National Association of Social Work .... www.naswdc.org

Sports

Coach Online Service .... www.coachhelp.com/jobs.htm
Cool Works .... www.coolworks.com
Fitness World Job Fair .... www.fitnessworld.com/pro/free/jobs.html
Online Sports
    Career Center .... www.onlinesports.com/pages/CareerCenter.html
Outdoor Jobnet .... www.outdoornetwork.com

Surveying

LandSurveyors.com .... www.landsurveyors.com

Technical

Water Resources
    Employment Opportunities .... www.uwin.siu.edu/announce/jobs

Truckers

Layover .... www.layover.com

Trucking

1-800-Drivers 1800drivers.com
Truck.net .... www.truck.net
truckers.com .... www.truckers.com

Utiliities

American Water Works Association .... www.awwa.org
ELECTRICJobs .... www.electricjobs.com
PMA Online .... www.powermarketers.com/main.htm
American Gas Association .... www.aga.com
Electric Power Newslink .... www.powermag.com
Electrical World .... www.electricalworld.com

Writing

The Write Jobs .... www.writerswrite.com/jobs

Zoo

Zoo Employment Listings .... www.aza.org/communique/positions

BUSINESS AND CAREER RESOURCES

Contact Impact Publications for a free annotated listing of resources or visit the World Wide Web for a complete listing of resources: www.impactpublications.com. The following books are available directly from Impact Publications. Complete the following form or list the titles, include postage (see formula at the end), enclose payment, and send your order to:

IMPACT PUBLICATIONS
9104 Manassas Drive, Suite N
Manassas Park, VA 20111-5211

Tel 1-800/361-1055, 703/361-7300, or Fax 703/335-9486

Quick and easy online ordering: *www.impactpublications.com*

Qty.	Titles	Price	Total
	BOOKS BY RAY SCHREYER AND JOHN McCARTER		
_____	The Best 100 Web Sites for HR Professionals	13.95	_____
_____	The Employer's Guide to Recruiting on the Internet	24.95	_____
_____	Recruit and Retain the Best	14.95	_____
	THE CAREERSAVVY SERIES		
_____	100 Top Internet Job Sites	12.95	_____
_____	101 Hiring Mistakes Employers Make...Avoid Them	14.95	_____
_____	Anger and Conflict in the Workplace	15.95	_____
_____	The Best 100 Web Sites for HR Professionals	13.95	_____
_____	The Difficult Hire	14.95	_____
_____	Recruit and Retain the Best	14.95	_____
_____	Savvy Interviewing	10.95	_____
_____	The Savvy Resume Writer	12.95	_____
	HIRING & RETENTION		
_____	45 Effective Ways for Hiring Smart!	24.95	_____
_____	96 Great Interview Questions to Ask Before You Hire	16.95	_____
_____	Ask the Right Questions, Hire the Best People	14.99	_____
_____	CareerXroads 2000	26.95	_____
_____	Complete Reference Checking Handbook	29.95	_____
_____	Directory of Executive Recruiters 2000	47.95	_____
_____	Employer's Guide to Recruiting on the Internet	24.95	_____
_____	Essential Book of Interviewing	15.00	_____
_____	Fast Forward MBA in Hiring	14.95	_____
_____	Finding and Keeping Great Employees	24.95	_____
_____	High Impact Hiring	34.95	_____
_____	Hire With Your Head	29.95	_____

Qty.	Titles	Price	Total
_____	Hiring: How to Find & Keep the Best People	12.99	_____
_____	Hiring and Managing Personnel Library	299.95	_____
_____	Love 'Em or Lose 'Em	17.95	_____
_____	Manager's Book of Questions	12.95	_____
_____	Smart Hiring	12.95	_____
_____	Smart Staffing	19.95	_____
_____	Unofficial Guide to Hiring & Firing Employees	16.00	_____
_____	Verify Those Credentials	19.95	_____
_____	Weddle's Guide to Employment Web-sites	21.95	_____

MOTIVATING & ENERGIZING YOUR WORKFORCE

Qty.	Titles	Price	Total
_____	1001 Ways to Energize Employees	12.00	_____
_____	1001 Ways to Reward Employees	12.00	_____
_____	A New Attitude	99.00	_____
_____	Attitude!	149.00	_____
_____	Bringing Out the Best in People	21.95	_____
_____	Dilbert Principle	20.00	_____
_____	Getting Employees to Fall in Love with Your Company	17.95	_____
_____	How to Be a Star at Work	12.00	_____
_____	Joy of Work	22.00	_____
_____	Motivating and Rewarding Employees	99.00	_____
_____	Motivation and Goal-Setting	99.00	_____
_____	Passionate Organization	24.95	_____
_____	Take This Job and Thrive	14.95	_____

INTERNET JOB SEARCH/HIRING

Qty.	Titles	Price	Total
_____	Career Exploration On the Internet	15.95	_____
_____	Electronic Resumes	19.95	_____
_____	Employer's Guide to Recruiting on the Internet	24.95	_____
_____	Guide to Internet Job Search.	14.95	_____
_____	Heart & Soul Internet Job Search	16.95	_____
_____	Internet Jobs Kit	149.95	_____
_____	Internet Resumes	14.95	_____
_____	Job Searching Online for Dummies	24.99	_____
_____	Resumes in Cyberspace	14.95	_____

ALTERNATIVE JOBS & EMPLOYERS

Qty.	Titles	Price	Total
_____	100 Best Careers for the 21st Century	15.95	_____
_____	100 Great Jobs and How To Get Them	17.95	_____
_____	101 Careers	16.95	_____
_____	150 Best Companies for Liberal Arts Graduates	15.95	_____
_____	50 Coolest Jobs in Sports	15.95	_____
_____	Adams Job Almanac 2000	16.95	_____
_____	American Almanac of Jobs and Salaries	20.00	_____
_____	Back Door Guide to Short-Term Job Adventures	19.95	_____
_____	Best Jobs for the 21st Century	19.95	_____
_____	Breaking & Entering	17.95	_____
_____	Careers in Computers	17.95	_____
_____	Careers in Health Care	17.95	_____
_____	Careers in High Tech	17.95	_____
_____	Career Smarts	12.95	_____
_____	College Not Required	12.95	_____
_____	Cool Careers for Dummies	16.95	_____

Qty.	Titles	Price	Total
_____	Cybercareers	24.95	_____
_____	Directory of Executive Recruiters	47.95	_____
_____	Flight Attendant Job Finder	16.95	_____
_____	Great Jobs Ahead	11.95	_____
_____	Health Care Job Explosion!	17.95	_____
_____	Hidden Job Market 2000	18.95	_____
_____	High-Skill, High-Wage Jobs	19.95	_____
_____	JobBank Guide to Computer and High-Tech Companies	16.95	_____
_____	JobSmarts Guide to Top 50 Jobs	15.00	_____
_____	Liberal Arts Jobs	14.95	_____
_____	Media Companies 2000	18.95	_____
_____	Quantum Companies II	26.95	_____
_____	Sunshine Jobs	16.95	_____
_____	Take It From Me	12.00	_____
_____	Top 100	19.95	_____
_____	Top 2,500 Employers 2000	18.95	_____
_____	Trends 2000	14.99	_____
_____	What Employers Really Want	14.95	_____
_____	Working in TV News	12.95	_____
_____	Workstyles to Fit Your Lifestyle	11.95	_____
_____	You Can't Play the Game If You Don't Know the Rules	14.95	_____

RECRUITERS/EMPLOYERS

Qty.	Titles	Price	Total
_____	Adams Executive Recruiters Almanac	16.95	_____
_____	Directory of Executive Recruiters 2000	47.95	_____
_____	Employer's Guide to Recruiting on the Internet	24.95	_____
_____	Job Seekers Guide to Executive Recruiters	34.95	_____
_____	Job Seekers Guide to Recruiters In. . .Series	36.95	_____

JOB STRATEGIES AND TACTICS

Qty.	Titles	Price	Total
_____	101 Ways to Power Up Your Job Search	12.95	_____
_____	110 Big Mistakes Job Hunters	19.95	_____
_____	24 Hours to Your Next Job, Raise, or Promotion	10.95	_____
_____	Better Book for Getting Hired	11.95	_____
_____	Career Bounce-Back	14.95	_____
_____	Career Chase	17.95	_____
_____	Career Fitness	19.95	_____
_____	Career Intelligence	15.95	_____
_____	Career Starter	10.95	_____
_____	Coming Alive From 9 to 5	18.95	_____
_____	Complete Idiot's Guide to Changing Careers	17.95	_____
_____	Executive Job Search Strategies	16.95	_____
_____	First Job Hunt Survival Guide	11.95	_____
_____	Five Secrets to Finding a Job	12.95	_____
_____	Get a Job You Love!	19.95	_____
_____	Get It Together By 30	14.95	_____
_____	Get the Job You Want Series	37.95	_____
_____	Get Ahead! Stay Ahead!	12.95	_____
_____	Getting from Fired to Hired	14.95	_____
_____	Great Jobs for Liberal Arts Majors	11.95	_____
_____	IIow to Get a Job in 90 Days or Less	12.95	_____
_____	How to Get Interviews from Classified Job Ads	14.95	_____
_____	How to Succeed Without a Career Path	13.95	_____
_____	How to Get the Job You Really Want	9.95	_____

Qty.	Titles	Price	Total
_____	How to Make Use of a Useless Degree	13.00	_____
_____	Is It Too Late To Run Away and Join the Circus?	14.95	_____
_____	Job Hunting in the 21st Century	17.95	_____
_____	Job Hunting for the Utterly Confused	14.95	_____
_____	Job Hunting Made Easy	12.95	_____
_____	Job Search: The Total System	14.95	_____
_____	Job Search Organizer	12.95	_____
_____	Job Search Time Manager	14.95	_____
_____	JobShift	13.00	_____
_____	JobSmart	12.00	_____
_____	Kiplinger's Survive and Profit From a Mid-Career Change	12.95	_____
_____	Knock 'Em Dead 2000	12.95	_____
_____	Me, Myself, and I, Inc.	17.95	_____
_____	New Rights of Passage	29.95	_____
_____	No One Is Unemployable	29.95	_____
_____	Not Just Another Job	12.00	_____
_____	Part-Time Careers	10.95	_____
_____	Perfect Job Search	12.95	_____
_____	Princeton Review Guide to Your Career	20.00	_____
_____	Perfect Pitch	13.99	_____
_____	Portable Executive	12.00	_____
_____	Professional's Job Finder	18.95	_____
_____	Reinventing Your Career	9.99	_____
_____	Resumes Don't Get Jobs	10.95	_____
_____	Right Fit	14.95	_____
_____	Right Place at the Right Time	11.95	_____
_____	Second Careers	14.95	_____
_____	Secrets from the Search Firm Files	24.95	_____
_____	So What If I'm 50	12.95	_____
_____	Staying in Demand	12.95	_____
_____	Strategic Job Jumping	13.00	_____
_____	SuccessAbilities	14.95	_____
_____	Take Yourself to the Top	13.99	_____
_____	Temping: The Insiders Guide	14.95	_____
_____	Top 10 Career Strategies for the Year 2000 & Beyond	12.00	_____
_____	Top 10 Fears of Job Seekers	12.00	_____
_____	Ultimate Job Search Survival	14.95	_____
_____	VGMs Career Checklist	9.95	_____
_____	Welcome to the Real World	13.00	_____
_____	What Do I Say Next?	20.00	_____
_____	What Employers Really Want	14.95	_____
_____	When Do I Start	11.95	_____
_____	Who Says There Are No Jobs Out There	12.95	_____
_____	Work Happy Live Healthy	14.95	_____
_____	Work This Way	14.95	_____
_____	You and Co., Inc.	22.00	_____
_____	Your Hidden Assets	19.95	_____

TESTING AND ASSESSMENT

_____	Career Counselor's Tool Kit	45.00	_____
_____	Career Discovery Project	12.95	_____
_____	Career Exploration Inventory	29.95	_____
_____	Career Satisfaction and Success	14.95	_____
_____	Career Tests	12.95	_____

Qty.	Titles	Price	Total
_____	Crystal-Barkley Guide to Taking Charge of Your Career	9.95	_____
_____	Dictionary of Holland Occupational Codes	45.00	_____
_____	Discover the Best Jobs For You	14.95	_____
_____	Discover What You're Best At	12.00	_____
_____	Gifts Differing	14.95	_____
_____	Have You Got What It Takes?	12.95	_____
_____	How to Find the Work You Love	10.95	_____
_____	Making Vocational Choices	29.95	_____
_____	New Quick Job Hunting Map	4.95	_____
_____	P.I.E. Method for Career Success	14.95	_____
_____	Putting Your Talent to Work	12.95	_____
_____	Real People, Real Jobs	15.95	_____
_____	Self-Directed Search and Related Holland Career Materials	27.95	_____
_____	Self-Directed Search Form R Combination Package	74.00	_____
_____	Starting Out, Starting Over	14.95	_____
_____	Test Your IQ	6.95	_____
_____	Three Boxes of Life	18.95	_____
_____	Type Talk	11.95	_____
_____	WORKTypes	12.99	_____

ATTITUDE & MOTIVATION

Qty.	Titles	Price	Total
_____	Ways to Motivate Yourself	15.99	_____
_____	Change Your Attitude	15.99	_____
_____	Reinventing Yourself	18.99	_____

INSPIRATION & EMPOWERMENT

Qty.	Titles	Price	Total
_____	10 Stupid Things Men Do to Mess Up Their Lives	13.00	_____
_____	10 Stupid Things Women Do	12.00	_____
_____	101 Great Resumes	9.99	_____
_____	101 Simple Ways to Be Good to Yourself	12.95	_____
_____	Awaken the Giant Within	12.00	_____
_____	Beating Job Burnout	12.95	_____
_____	Big Things Happen When You Do the Little Things Right	15.00	_____
_____	Career Busters	10.95	_____
_____	Chicken Soup for the Soul Series	87.95	_____
_____	Do What You Love, the Money Will Follow	11.95	_____
_____	Doing It All Isn't Everything	19.95	_____
_____	Doing Work You Love	14.95	_____
_____	Emotional Intelligence	13.95	_____
_____	First Things First	23.00	_____
_____	Get What You Deserve	23.00	_____
_____	Getting Unstuck	11.99	_____
_____	If It's Going To Be, It's Up To Me	22.00	_____
_____	If Life Is A Game, These Are the Rules	15.00	_____
_____	In Search of Values	8.99	_____
_____	Job/Family Challenge: A 9-5 Guide	12.95	_____
_____	Kick In the Seat of the Pants	11.95	_____
_____	Kiplinger's Taming the Paper Tiger	11.95	_____
_____	Life Skills	17.95	_____
_____	Love Your Work and Success Will Follow	12.95	_____
_____	Path, The	14.95	_____
_____	Personal Job Power	12.95	_____
_____	Power of Purpose	20.00	_____

Qty.	Titles	Price	Total
_____	Seven Habits of Highly Effective People	14.00	_____
_____	Softpower	10.95	_____
_____	Stop Postponing the Rest of Your Life	9.95	_____
_____	Suvivor Personality	12.00	_____
_____	To Build the Life You Want, Create the Work You Love	10.95	_____
_____	Unlimited Power	12.00	_____
_____	Wake-Up Calls	18.95	_____
_____	Your Signature Path	24.95	_____

RESUMES & LETTERS

Qty.	Titles	Price	Total
_____	$110,000 Resume	16.95	_____
_____	100 Winning Resumes for $100,000+ Jobs	24.95	_____
_____	101 Best Resumes	10.95	_____
_____	101 More Best Resumes	11.95	_____
_____	101 Quick Tips for a Dynamite Resume	13.95	_____
_____	1500+ Key Words for 100,000+	14.95	_____
_____	175 High-Impact Resumes	10.95	_____
_____	Adams Resume Almanac/Disk	19.95	_____
_____	America's Top Resumes for America's Top Jobs	19.95	_____
_____	Asher's Bible of Exec.utive Resumes	29.95	_____
_____	Best Resumes for $75,000+ Executive Jobs	14.95	_____
_____	Best Resumes for Attorneys	16.95	_____
_____	Better Resumes in Three Easy Steps	12.95	_____
_____	Blue Collar and Beyond	8.95	_____
_____	Blue Collar Resumes	11.99	_____
_____	Building a Great Resume	15.00	_____
_____	Complete Idiot's Guide to Writing the Perfect Resume	16.95	_____
_____	Conquer Resume Objections	10.95	_____
_____	Creating Your High School Resume and Portfolio	13.90	_____
_____	Creating Your Skills Portfolio	10.95	_____
_____	Cyberspace Resume Kit	16.95	_____
_____	Damn Good Resume Guide	12.95	_____
_____	Dynamite Resumes	14.95	_____
_____	Edge Resume and Job Search Strategy	23.95	_____
_____	Electronic Resumes and Onlline Networking	13.99	_____
_____	Encyclopedia of Job-Winning Resumes	16.95	_____
_____	Gallery of Best Resumes	16.95	_____
_____	Gallery of Best Resumes for Two-Year Degree Graduates	16.95	_____
_____	Heart & Soul Resumes	15.95	_____
_____	High Impact Resumes and Letters	19.95	_____
_____	How to Prepare Your Curriculum Vitae	14.95	_____
_____	Just Resumes	11.95	_____
_____	New Perfect Resume	10.95	_____
_____	Overnight Resume	12.95	_____
_____	Portfolio Power	14.95	_____
_____	Power Resumes	14.95	_____
_____	Prof. Resumes/Executives, Managers, & Other Administrators	19.95	_____
_____	Quick Resume and Cover Letter Book	12.95	_____
_____	Ready-To-Go Resumes	29.95	_____
_____	Resume Catalog	15.95	_____
_____	Resume Magic	18.95	_____
_____	Resume Power	12.95	_____
_____	Resume Pro	24.95	_____
_____	Resume Shortcuts	14.95	_____

Qty.	Titles	Price	Total
_____	Resume Writing Made Easy	11.95	_____
_____	Resumes for High School Grads.	9.95	_____
_____	Resumes for the Over-50 Job Hunter	14.95	_____
_____	Resumes for Re-Entry	10.95	_____
_____	Resume Winners from the Pros	17.95	_____
_____	Resumes for Dummies	12.99	_____
_____	Resumes for the Health Care Professional	14.95	_____
_____	Resumes, Resumes, Resumes	9.99	_____
_____	Resumes That Knock 'Em Dead	10.95	_____
_____	Resumes That Will Get You the Job You Want	12.99	_____
_____	Savvy Resume Writer	10.95	_____
_____	Sure-Hire Resumes	14.95	_____
_____	Winning Resumes	10.95	_____
_____	Wow! Resumes	63.95	_____
_____	Your First Resume	9.99	_____
_____	Your Resume	24.95	_____

COVER LETTERS

Qty.	Titles	Price	Total
_____	101 Best Cover Letters	11.95	_____
_____	175 High-Impact Cover Letters	10.95	_____
_____	200 Letters for Job Hunters	19.95	_____
_____	201 Winning Cover Letters for the $100,000+ Jobs	24.95	_____
_____	201 Dynamite Job Search Letters	19.95	_____
_____	201 Killer Cover Letters	16.95	_____
_____	Complete Idiot's Guide to the Perfect Cover Letters	14.95	_____
_____	Cover Letters, Cover Letters, Cover Letters	9.99	_____
_____	Cover Letters for Dummies	12.99	_____
_____	Cover Letters that Knock 'Em Dead	10.95	_____
_____	Cover Letters That Will Get You the Job You Want	12.99	_____
_____	Dynamite Cover Letters	14.95	_____
_____	Gallery of Best Cover Letters	18.95	_____
_____	Haldane's Best Cover Letters for Professionals	15.95	_____
_____	Perfect Cover Letter	10.95	_____
_____	Winning Cover Letters	10.95	_____

ETIQUETTE AND IMAGE

Qty.	Titles	Price	Total
_____	Business Etiquette and Professionalism	10.95	_____
_____	Dressing Smart in the New Millennium	15.95	_____
_____	Executive Etiquette in the New Workplace	14.95	_____
_____	First Five Minutes	14.95	_____
_____	John Molloy's Dress for Success (For Men)	13.99	_____
_____	Lions Don't Need to Roar	10.99	_____
_____	New Professional Image	12.95	_____
_____	New Women's Dress for Success	12.99	_____
_____	Red Socks Don't Work	14.95	_____
_____	Successful Style	17.95	_____
_____	VGMs Complete Guide to Career Etiquette	12.95	_____
_____	Winning Image	17.95	_____
_____	You've Only Got 3 Seconds	22.95	_____

INTERVIEWING: JOBSEEKERS

Qty.	Titles	Price	Total
_____	101 Dynamite Answers to Interview Questions	12.95	_____
_____	101 Dynamite Questions to Ask at Your Job Interview	14.95	_____

Qty.	Titles	Price	Total
_____	101 Tough Interview Questions. . .	14.95	_____
_____	111 Dynamite Ways to Ace Your Job Interview	13.95	_____
_____	Best Answers/201 Most Frequently Asked Interview Questions	10.95	_____
_____	Complete Q & A Job Interview Book	14.95	_____
_____	Conquer Interview Objectives	10.95	_____
_____	Get Hired	14.95	_____
_____	Haldane's Best Answers to Tough Interview Questions	15.95	_____
_____	Information Interviewing	10.95	_____
_____	Interview for Success	15.95	_____
_____	Interview Strategies ThatWill Get You the Job You Want	12.99	_____
_____	Interview Power	12.95	_____
_____	Job Interviews for Dummies	12.99	_____
_____	Job Interviews That Mean Business	12.00	_____
_____	Killer Interviews	10.95	_____
_____	Savvy Interviewer	10.95	_____
_____	Successful Interviewing for College Seniors	11.95	_____
_____	Sweaty Palms	8.95	_____
_____	Your First Interview	9.95	_____

NETWORKING

Qty.	Titles	Price	Total
_____	52 Ways to Re-Connect, Follow Up, and Stay in Touch	14.95	_____
_____	Dig Your Well Before You're Thirsty	24.95	_____
_____	Dynamite Networking for Dynamite Jobs	15.95	_____
_____	Dynamite Tele-Search	12.95	_____
_____	Effective Networking	10.95	_____
_____	Golden Rule of Schmoozing	12.95	_____
_____	Great Connections	11.95	_____
_____	How to Work a Room	11.99	_____
_____	Network Your Way to Success	19.95	_____
_____	Networking for Everyone	16.95	_____
_____	People Power	14.95	_____
_____	Power Networking	14.95	_____
_____	Power Schmoozing	12.95	_____
_____	Power To Get In	24.95	_____

SALARY NEGOTIATIONS

Qty.	Titles	Price	Total
_____	Dynamite Salary Negotiations	15.95	_____
_____	Get a Raise in 7 Days	14.95	_____
_____	Get More Money on Your Next Job	14.95	_____
_____	Negotiate Your Job Offer	14.95	_____

ENTREPRENEURS AND CONSULTANTS

Qty.	Titles	Price	Total
_____	10 Hottest Consulting Practices	27.95	_____
_____	101 Best Businesses to Start	17.50	_____
_____	101 Best Home Businesses	14.99	_____
_____	101 Best Weekend Businesses	14.99	_____
_____	555 Ways to Earn Extra Money	12.95	_____
_____	Adams Businesses You Can Start Almanac	14.95	_____
_____	Adams Streetwise Small Business Start-Up	16.95	_____
_____	Adams Streetwise Small Business Start-Up CD-ROM	59.95	_____
_____	Be Your Own Business	12.95	_____
_____	Best Home-Based Businesses for the 90s	12.95	_____

Qty.	Titles	Price	Total
_____	Consultant's Proposal, Fee, and Contract Problem-Solver	19.95	_____
_____	Discovering Your Career in Business (With Disk)	22.00	_____
_____	Finding Your Perfect Work	16.95	_____
_____	Franchise Opportunities Handbook	16.95	_____
_____	Getting Business to Come to You CD-ROM	49.95	_____
_____	How to Raise a Family and Career Under One Roof	15.95	_____
_____	How to Really Start Your Own Business	19.95	_____
_____	How to Start, Run, and Stay in Business	14.95	_____
_____	Howto Succeed as an Independent Consultant	29.95	_____
_____	How to Start and Run a Successful Consulting Business	15.95	_____
_____	Ideal Entrepreneurial Business For You	16.95	_____
_____	Joining the Entrepreneurial Elite	25.95	_____
_____	NBEW's Guide to Self-Employment	12.95	_____
_____	Selling on the Internet	24.95	_____
_____	Start-Up	16.99	_____
_____	Starting on a Shoestring	16.95	_____
_____	Winning Government Contracts	19.95	_____

☞ **SUBTOTAL** $ _____

☞ Virginia residents add 4½% sales tax) _____

☞ Shipping/handling, Continental U.S., $5.00 + _____ $5.00
plus following percentages when **SUBTOTAL** is:

☐ $30-$100—multiply SUBTOTAL by 8%

☐ $100-$999—multiply SUBTOTAL by 7% _____

☐ $1,000-$4,999—multiply SUBTOTAL by 6% _____

☐ Over $5,000—multiply SUBTOTAL by 5% _____

☞ ☐ If shipped outside Continental US, add another 5% _____

☞ **TOTAL ENCLOSED** $_____

SHIP TO: (street address only for UPS or RPS delivery)

Name _____

Address _____

_____

_____

Telephone _____

I enclose ❑ Check ❑ Money Order in the amount of: $ _____

Charge $ _____ to ❑ Visa ❑ MC ❑ AmEx

Card # _____ Exp: _____ / _____

Signature _____

DISCOVER HUNDREDS OF ADDITIONAL RESOURCES ON THE WORLD WIDE WEB!

Looking for the newest and best books, directories, newsletters, wall charts, training programs, videos, computer software, and kits to help you energize your employees, effectively address sexual harassment issues, or improve your networking skills? Want to learn the most effective way to find a job in Asia or relocate to San Francisco? Are you curious about how to recruit a new employee using the Internet or about what you'll be doing five years from now? Are you trying to keep up-to-date on the latest HR resources, but are not able to find the latest catalogs, brochures, or newsletters on today's "best of the best" resources?

Welcome to the first virtual career bookstore on the Internet. Now you're only a click away with Impact Publications' electronic solution to the resource challenge. Visit this rich site to quickly discover everything you ever wanted to know about workplace diversity, career development, and compensation and benefits—including many useful resources that are difficult to find in local bookstores and libraries. The site also includes what's new and hot, tips for job search success, and monthly specials. Check it out today!

www.impactpublications.com

Don't be kept in the dark...
Sign Up For Impact's *FREE* E-Zine Today!

Get the latest information and special discounts on career, business, and travel products through our new electronic magazine (e-zine). Becoming a member of this exclusive "What's New and Special" group is quick and easy. Just enter your email address online on our Web site:

www.impactpublications.com

Or, email your email address to joinlist@impactpublications.com, or fax it to (703/335-9486).

Impact Publications ◆ 9104 Manassas Drive, Suite N ◆ Manassas Park, VA 20111-5211 ◆ 703/361-7300 ◆ www.impactpublications.com